# About the Author

Born in Lancashire, mill town of Oldham, in the 1960s, Don was of a generation and a culture where it was essential to grow 'big and strong', which meant eating as much as you could cram down your throat. This invariably led to him becoming a fatty. Having lost weight and kept it off, this smug bastard thought it would be a good idea to share his 'life of fat' with you and maybe you could also be a smug bastard!

# Wake Up, Fatty!

Donald N Sinclair

# Wake Up, Fatty!

Olympia Publishers
*London*

www.olympiapublishers.com
OLYMPIA PAPERBACK EDITION

Copyright © Donald N Sinclair 2018

The right of Donald N Sinclair to be identified as author of this work has been asserted in accordance with sections 77 and 78 of the Copyright, Designs and Patents Act 1988.

**All Rights Reserved**

No reproduction, copy or transmission of this publication may be made without written permission.
No paragraph of this publication may be reproduced, copied or transmitted save with the written permission of the publisher, or in accordance with the provisions of the Copyright Act 1956 (as amended).

Any person who commits any unauthorised act in relation to this publication may be liable to criminal prosecution and civil claims for damage.

A CIP catalogue record for this title is available from the British Library.

ISBN: 978-1-78830-184-8

First Published in 2018

Olympia Publishers
60 Cannon Street
London
EC4N 6NP

Printed in Great Britain

# Dedication

To my wife, Harriet, and sons, Jack and Joey

# INTRODUCTION

'Wake up, Fatty!' The term 'fatty' has been one of mockery throughout the last number of years. In my lifetime, a UK chart hit entitled *'Lip Up Fatty'* became part of everyday life. The record was performed by a band, fronted by a jolly, overweight skinhead, who, on the face of it seemed to revel in the sheer joy of his excessive body weight. At this particular time in my life, I, too, was carrying excessive bulk and, as was fashionable in the North West of England at the time, sported a crew cut. My best mate and I, who, at the time were both in apprenticeships, were working on the refurbishment of the exterior of a bank in Middleton, Greater Manchester. Our working platform was a scaffold, which was erected on the pavement adjoining a main road by a set of traffic lights. On one memorable occasion, a double-decker bus pulled up alongside our platform, giving us a perfect vantage of the top deck and its occupants as well as affording them the same sight line. The top deck was full of school children, who, on seeing me, started to chant almost in unison 'Lip Up Fatty!' This not only resulted in hilarity for all the kids on the top deck, resulting from my angry reaction, it also resulted in my work mates roaring with laughter and using the phrase as often as possible as a general 'put-down'. The year was 1980 and I was eighteen years old. For me, as you will gather from the rest of the book, I had been subjected to taunts regarding my weight since being at primary school. In today's politically correct society, my issues would probably be diagnosed as manic depression, brought on by bullying and my parents would have been at school, speaking with councillors in a bid to get to the root of the problem and make my life fulfilling and aspirational. As it was at the time, if I am being completely honest, the root cause of my problem was that I ate and drank too much of the wrong stuff and it was really down to my consumption and, as I will discuss later, it was society as a whole, that was driving my concerns It has taken me around four years to get my collective thoughts into this book, during which time I have studied, not only the philosophy of fat in some detail, but have questioned most things about the society we live in, as portrayed to me by the media from which I consume it. When I say 'study', I cannot pretend for one minute that I have attended any kind of academic programme. Moreover, I have reflected on my life experience while observing others, both in the flesh and in the media. We are told that a large proportion of the world's population are starving and that this issue is only going to get worse in the coming years due to the world's population increasing. Yet we are also told that, we, in the West (when I refer to 'we', I am generally speaking from a UK perspective) eat too much, as well as throwing away untenable amounts of food, whilst in the meantime, we are told, we are getting fatter and fatter. Looking objectively at the situation, it could be surmised that the West is a greedy, selfish, and wasteful entity, which is consuming both it and the rest of the world to death. As you walk down the street of any UK town, city or village, you will see that fat has become the norm. People who would, only thirty or forty years ago, have been mocked for their appearance go about their lives portraying a certain amount of confidence, as in my opinion, they are becoming less and less of a minority as their life unfolds. It is only my observation, however, when I think of really, really fat people, I tend to imagine someone who is working class and generally female, although, do not get me wrong, males are not immune from this epidemic. Of late, I have been spending some time working away from home. As a younger man, I enjoyed being out and about. However, now I am older, I yearn to be at home. During most weekday evenings, as is the case with most journeymen, I spend my time in public houses or restaurants, if for no other reason but to kill time before bed. As I write, my recent forays into the public house scene has seen me frequenting a 'chain' pub in a city in the South West of England. By chain pub I am referring to a pub owned by a large organisation who provide drink at a fraction of the cost of smaller pub owners and who serve food, at what appears to be ridiculously low prices. The pub is frequented by some of the fattest women I have ever seen, who, as a general observation also, without exception, have their children with them. Please do not get me wrong, I'm sure that the people in question are perfect parents and I can confirm that the regulars in the pub are great people (having chatted with a number of them). However, the whole scene makes me analyse the business model of the chain, trying to imagine how their business model works. It is abundantly clear that, as a business, the chain has an overriding objective to maximise profitability. I imagine that they utilise economies of scale to provide almost out of date beer and low-quality food at a price range which suits the spending capacity of their target market, whilst at the same time, paying as little as possible to people of a similar ilk to serve this shit to them. When one starts to look at the business model in these terms, it is easy to surmise that the people in the model don't really count. Well, not in the caring, humanistic way the chain would have you believe. The people only count, if they appear in droves, continually eating and drinking the cheap, mass-produced shit you are able to provide them. I often wonder if the people who sit on the boards of these organisations rush out on a Tuesday evening because it's 'Steak Night'? This phenomenon of cheap, shit food can be seen up and down the UK, in public places as well as the home. How many times have you been to a carvery? This concept is another example of mass-marketed gluttony, where people stand in line waiting to get as much meat as possible given to them by someone with a large knife and a chef's hat. On receipt of the long awaited flesh, which, if you are very lucky, will include large portions of more than one type of meat, the recipient will then proceed to the 'help yourself' section of the ceremony, whereby they, in eager anticipation of the feast ahead, stack their plate with enough food to feed a village! At such an event, it is not uncommon for the attendees to repeat the process. This, from a consumer's perspective, it seems, results in good value for money. I would agree that it is good value. However, the main beneficiary is the organisation selling the shit to the 'lemmings' that consume it! If we are to believe that we are getting fatter through lifestyle and overeating, then the ceremony of carveries, steak night, pie night and whatever other media for selling shite to the masses would be questioned and probably require a health warning, similar to the ones displayed on cartons of cigarettes, if we were the 'caring society' that we all perceive ourselves to be. It is my humble opinion that the general populist is being 'sold a pup'. Everybody, from no matter which class (don't get me started on the class system), aspires to live like royalty; and corporations and those who depend on the masses for their very existence, continually improve on the way in which they provide access to these aspirations. Christmas is a particularly good time to observe this philosophy in action. What I imagine to have been a period of spiritual reflection, arising from the birth of a well- known Christian prophet, has, in my opinion, become an opportunity for the shit sellers to tap into the greed and gluttony which perpetuates in our society, by selling us concepts such as 'the party season'. In summary, so I am led to believe, the party season is when it is imperative that you wear your best clothes (new, of course, to impress your peers) and to hold a lavish party, utilising the services of a well-known corporation who specialises in knocking out frozen party platters, containing all manner of exotic, interesting and delicious delights. Again, looking at it from the corporate perspective, the new clothes were probably made in a sweatshop in somewhere like Bangladesh for a few pennies and the food mass produced in a Malaysian factory, which probably makes animal feed during the aftermath of Christmas. I often wonder how the workers in the food processing plant perceive the recipients of the slop that they produce; and I conclude that they probably concur with my opinion that our gluttony masks the fact that, if we are told that what we are eating is delicious and exclusive, then we would eat frozen dog shit just to live up to the aspirations which are sold to us in the first place!

Eating and drinking are essential to our very existence. These functions are what keep us alive. During a recent news story, a group of people who had been fleeing conflict in some Middle Eastern conflict zone, came out of their hiding place in some wooded, or mountainous area. They had been hiding for a number of weeks. The harrowing tale, went on to describe how they had gathered dew from leaves to drink and ate plants and leaves for sustenance. This, in my opinion, is eating and drinking undertaken for its very purpose, to live. We in the West, on the other hand, have unfettered access to food and drink, with the net result being a gold-plated opportunity for corporations and businesses to sell us lifestyle choices and aspirations. The net result of this, based purely on my life experiences and observations, is that we will consume! As I write and as is well portrayed in the media, we in the West are in the middle of, what is sold to us as an obesity crisis, to which, guess what? The corporations, tapping into the new-found aspiration not to be a fatty, are knocking out the answers to all our problems, which, you guessed it, is more slop, sold at a premium; resulting in corporate profits. Before I end this introduction, I must recall an actual international occurrence which caused some bitterness between Germany and Holland in the 1990s. Holland, at the time, produced large amounts of fruit and vegetables (when I say Holland, I probably should say a Dutch corporation) with large quantities being exported to Germany. There had been some political dispute arising from the quality and cost of these imports and this issue had raised itself to the profile of the higher echelons of the governments of both countries. Now, I'm not sure I have the quote exactly right, however, the Dutch Minister in question (probably the agriculture minister) made a statement similar to the following: 'Feed the swill to the pigs!' As you can imagine, this caused uproar in Germany, as I bore witness as I was there at the time. However, the sentiment stuck with me, that producing food for the masses is exactly like, from a corporate perspective, producing swill for pigs. If you can feed the pigs the cheapest shit possible, once slaughtered, you will have minimised your unit costs and maximised your profits. I get frustrated by the constant reassurance that our leaders and politicians have our best interests at heart; a sentiment that, if you look at what they actually say and do, is proven, on the whole, not to be the case. Even our great leaders, the ones who have had statues commissioned have dropped their guard on numerous occasions. Take Churchill, for example. On an occasion, when faced with an issue arising from a miners' strike, he was heard to proclaim: (again, I might have this quote slightly wrong, but you will get the jist) 'Send those rats back down their holes!' What a hero!

# WHEN DID YOU GET FAT?

Many people around the world are vastly overweight. Perhaps you are one of them? Perhaps you have purchased or borrowed this book in the hope that you will lose the fat? I, as I will bang on about on numerous occasions below, have been overweight during two specific periods of my life and on both occasions, have managed to lose the fat. On the second occasion, which is the current phase of my life, I have managed to maintain the weight that I want for about two years. It's important for all to know, however, that I view being a fatty in the same way any alcoholic would view alcoholism, in that, just as an alcoholic refrains from consuming alcohol to control his or her addiction, I choose to refrain from certain types and quantities of food and food types at certain times. Make no mistake, losing weight and particularly, maintaining the weight that you desire, is not something that comes naturally to me. I will explain below my thought processes and the way in which I consider that civilisation, in its current form influences, not only our propensity to get fat, but also our perceived inability to take control of our lifestyles. Before I explore the issue in more detail, I think it's important for everybody, if they are going to lose the weight, to take a moment to think back and identify the exact point in their lives where they, alone in the world, realised that they were fat. I am not any sort of esteemed paediatric consultant, however, I think it's pretty safe to state that nobody is born chronically obese. It follows and again, it is I would say, pretty safe to conclude that societal influences, both peer influences and parental influences, on an individual can result in the production of a fatty. No one, as far as I am aware, unless they are planning a circus career, sets out to be a fatty. People just go about their normal lives, consume what they consume and at some point realise that they are fat.

For me, the first realisation that I was fat came in the early 1970s when I was about nine years old. I was born and raised in the Lancashire mill town of Oldham and lived in, what was for Oldham, a reasonably respectable area. I suppose the time in question may have had some bearing on my food consumption, as well as the working class culture that pervaded at the time. My parents, who were born in the 1940s were, as has become known, 'baby boomers', having been raised during war time and with food rationing. The post war period saw an abundance of previously unavailable, or difficult to obtain, foods and consumables which were consumed, it appears, with relish by one and all. Interestingly enough, televisions became more and more part of peoples' lives during this very same period, which, as I will discuss later, started to significantly influence the population's behaviours and aspirations. In short, as a small child the culture was to consume whatever was put on your plate, until your plate was empty, otherwise you would be in trouble. Now, I am at pains to stress that I do not, in any way, blame my parents for over-feeding me, as they had been raised in a time of severe austerity and it's only natural to want to 'do the best for your kids'. However, my issue with regards that time, just as today, is the source of knowledge with regards how to do the best for your kids; the sources being television, newspapers, and the media in general, which, today of course, includes social media. It's a kind of paradox that individualistic activities, such as sitting in front of a personal computer (the word 'personal' being the key here) can, in effect, make the individual part of the herd. I can picture in my mind's eye a photograph of me, aged about six years old. I was a pageboy at my auntie's wedding. The picture is of me, handing her a 'lucky' black cat. For me, the striking relevance of this photograph is that I am not fat. I have looked at other photographs of me as a child and it is clear to see that I definitely am fat. Over the years and of course during the thought processes behind this book, I have tried to 'pin down' the 'when and why', with regards to me becoming a fatty. I attended a Church of England primary school and just like many, if not all, of the children at the time, was subjected to school dinners. It's worth noting at this stage that every school day started at home with a breakfast which was consumed at about 8am. A couple of hours later, milk and biscuits and I remember my favourites being Jammy Dodgers. Life at primary school during that time could be summarised, particularly if your first name was Donald, as 'be bullied, or fight back'. It was unfortunate that at the time I shared my Christian name with a very famous cartoon duck. On hearing my name, it was often common for children and adults (including teachers) to make reference to the aforementioned bird. There was a rhyme, which was used generally by children, which went: (I remember every word)

Donald Duck, did some muck,
Upon the kitchen floor.
Mrs Duck, wiped it up
And Donald did some more.

This rhyme has stuck with me since as early as I can remember in my life as boys and girls alike, alone, but more often in groups, used to chant the rhyme over and over again, with me at the time feeling helpless and often isolated. The chanting was often, in the early days, a precursor to some kind of scuffle, which would more often than not result in me getting in trouble or being branded as a bully. Imagine a similar scene today, with the liberal 'namby–pamby' brigade; such behaviour would warrant an appearance on the local television news! But for me, I had the wise words of my mother, telling me to hit them back or the relentless mockery would never stop. As a small child, I remember the sentiment of my parents and my grandmother being along the lines of 'eat your food then you will grow up to be big and strong'. For me, this correlated to 'the more you eat, the bigger and stronger you will get'. Having a 'healthy appetite' also carried favour with adults and during school dinner, it was not uncommon for me to consume second and third helpings of the slop they provided. A particular foodstuff which sticks in my mind is mashed potato, which was dispensed in blobs by a stainless-steel dispenser and which, as it was plopped onto your plate, was given a number and referred to as a 'blob of mash'. Utilising the ability to consume more than one portion, it was not uncommon for me to devour 10 – 15 blobs of mash in one sitting. As you can imagine, it wasn't long before the weight started to appear. Out of school, I led a very active social life, playing out on the street with numerous other kids in the area. One particular peer group I belonged to included my mates who were identical twins, who, to say the least were rogues, having a reputation across a large geographical area for being 'hard'. The twins were about three years older than me and it has to be said were indulged to the extreme by their mother, who provided them with what appeared to me at the time, with everything you would ever need. So, at the age of nine, in this particular peer group (they lived about five doors down the street from me), I hung out and aspired to the same aspirations as a group of 12-year-olds. The twins' father had built them a shed adjacent to their house which, as you will imagine, quickly became a smoking and drinking hide-out, which, became attractive to older kids, of about 15-16. So, on any given night, the shed would be occupied with a group of kids aged from 9 up to 16, who would sit, huddled around a pot-bellied stove (installed by the twins' father) smoking, drinking and swearing. They would, on occasion, would go out into the local area and 'raise hell'. On one particular occasion, in around 1971, I remember it was hot and we were playing football with our shirts off and that's when it happened. One of the 16-year-olds gave me a look of distain and a remark which stays with me to this day: 'Ooooh, look at that fat!' He was referring to my upper torso. For me, this was an event that switched off my inhibitions and made me self-conscious to the point that still to this day, I am loath to reveal my torso to anybody.

As for the 16-year-old (who will remain nameless), I often wonder where he is now as I'm convinced he was some kind of prat. I often ask myself 'what kind of 16-year-old hangs around with primary school children?' I'll let you provide the answers to that question! I did actually have occasion, nine years later, to interface with the prick again for a period of time. At this time, I was now over six feet tall and weighing about 19 stones. I wasn't exactly what you would call a 'hard-case', however, I found that size was a great intimidator, in the case of the prat in question. I recall on one occasion us 'squaring up' at a local village country club I often used to frequent, but, as with most scuffles, nothing significant was sorted out. I guess I still had the grudge and he couldn't accept the fact that I was now an adult. He very soon got banned from the country club, due to the fact that he threw a pint pot across the room. I am, to this day convinced that the pint pot was destined for me. However, the prat launched it into the face of a young woman who was sat amongst a group of her friends, resulting in mass hysteria and blood. That was the last I ever saw of the prat.

Returning to me as a nine-year-old and moving on through primary and secondary school, the eating ruse kind of backfired, in that now, not only was I 'Donald Duck', I was now a fatty and although I could more than defend myself against the bullies, I had difficulty in catching them due to my bulk impeding my ability to run! An interesting issue for me at this stage is, looking back I remember realising that I was fat, after all, I was reminded constantly by the taunts of others. However, I don't remember, as a youngster, being motivated to do anything about it. I was resigned to the fact that I was a fatty and had no perception that I should really do something about it. I just shrugged off the bullies to the point that my resultant behaviour probably resulted in my bullying others. I do remember, however, a mantra that my Father repeated to me often: 'Fat boys make fat men'. I remember hearing this and worrying somehow, that I was going to be a 'fat man'. Sure enough, as I will discuss later, I changed my eating habits and lost a pile of weight.

You will note above that I referred to my tormenters as 'bullies'. Bullying, in today's liberal, Western society has become a phrase behind which certain members of society can hide; to allow them to be insulting or disparaging towards, or about, someone, without them appearing to be the prick that they actually are. By labelling someone a bully; sexist; racist; or homophobic, prior to a verbal assault, has become culturally acceptable, or so it seems, to accept that that person is a 'bad person'; regardless of whether they are any of those things or not. Please don't misinterpret my point here, I consider myself to be none of those things. However, you only need to watch the television to see that a cultural pattern has emerged, used predominantly by the politicians, the media and those who consider themselves to be artists. By labelling someone first and establishing that they are (oh dear, there is only one word I can use here) a cunt, then you feel somehow you are doing the world a favour by pointing out their misgivings, usually to illustrate what a fantastic person you are. Seen recently during the 2016 American General Election, the two presidential candidates utilised vast resources to dig up instances of what is considered to be unacceptable behaviour, in order to present themselves as 'holier than thou'. Recently, I was shown a text message, sent to one of my in-laws, which, using the exact same formula, described my character traits in, let's say, an unfavourable light. What I found interesting was the phrase, 'Donald is a bully, and I've heard other people in the family say this too'. The second part of that statement was the protagonist's justification, it is fair to assume, to justify their behaviour. As if to say, 'well, although during this rant I'm unable to pinpoint an exact instance of bullying, I have it on good authority, from a relative, who shall remain nameless that, he is indeed a bully. Therefore, I am now justified to continue with the bullying label, it having been fully established. Needless to say, I'm not a big fan of this particular person. However, the point I wanted to make and will continue to make later on, is that Western culture has defined ways in which to label individuals, or groups of people, who, once the label has been established, can be bad-mouthed at will, with the bad-mouther being free to continue with their bile, safe in the knowledge that they themselves can take the moral high ground. Fatties fall into the labelled category, and although our PC culture would not allow out-and-out verbal condemnation of them, the very way in which they are portrayed, or more often, not portrayed speaks volumes in terms of the way in which our culture treats them.

As you will read later on, I have had two occasions to lose weight, the first as an angst-ridden teenager, the second is the catalyst to my writing this book. But remember the question, one which I feel is very important? When did you realise you were fat? On my second, I'll call it an epiphany, I was at a wedding party. During this time in my life, I had spent a period at college and had just landed myself what I considered to be the ultimate job. The job in question was with my local authority working in the 'Highways and Property Department' as a Senior Technical Officer. Now, for anyone who has worked in the public sector, you will note that your job, due to cuts in public sector spending, is now constantly at risk. However, in 1996, which is the year in question in this instance, a job in the public sector was a job for life. I was amazed at the working conditions, which included flexi time, paid sick leave for months on end and a pension, which it turns out is 'gold plated' and underwritten by the tax payer. I had arrived! At the wedding party, I was wearing a blue woollen suit which I had bought on HP from a catalogue. I still have the suit now, 20 years later and it is massive. However, with a blue striped shirt (18 ½ neck) and a paisley tie, I felt the 'bees knees'; until a friend of the family, who I had not seen for a few years, asked what was for me at the time a very seminal question: 'When did that happen?' I was confused, so sought clarification. 'You getting so fat.' This for me was the killer statement and the realisation that once again, having lost loads of weight previously in my life, I was indeed a fatty. Adults, as we all know are far more sensitive to other people's predicaments than children, or teenagers. As a young fatty, my peers reminded me all the time of my fatness. Adults, on the other hand, in my experience, don't possess the inhibitions, so therefore this particular instance was seminal, and brought back, in an instance, all the anxieties I carried as a younger person. It is true to say, as an adult I was much more comfortable in my fat suit than I was when I was younger, as the distractions of parenthood and paying the mortgage took precedence over my appearance. However, it was always there and was something that I felt I needed to take control of at some time in the future. That future has happened, for me and I'm sure that, if you, as a fatty are looking to do something about it, you are in exactly the same position that I was. An important issue to note, however, and this is something that I will probably repeat over and over, it is not just overeating that is the problem, in my opinion. Well, it is overeating and drinking, but your perception of how you fit into society and how you, yourself deal with your personal issues is as important to you being the shape that you want to be. At the time of writing this chapter (it has taken me over three years to write this book), I am in the process of reading John Lydon's autobiography, '*Anger is an Energy*'. John Lydon, or as some people refer to him, 'Johnny Rotten', has been an inspiration to me throughout the years, in that the persona he portrays is that of a 'hater'. Having looked at myself during the writing of this book, I too believe that I fall into the 'hater' category. Please don't get me wrong, I don't hate everybody and everything. Moreover, I look for explanations and truth in everything. I don't believe for one minute that things just happen. By things I mean world events, such as wars, fashions and what is spewed out of the daily rags as 'being important'. It is my strong belief, that if you can, get some kind of understanding that the mantra of the advertising world, 'you're worth it', is a way of getting you to buy their unnecessary shit, or that the TV presenter bitch, with the six-pack has only made the exercise video to make money, then you are well on your way to taking control of your life and, in the context of this book, your weight. It seems that in particular, the lower down the food chain you go, in financial terms, the more people are dependent on 'the circus' to manage their everyday affairs. Their only solace derives from family values, as best displayed in the famous pop song '*Living in the love of the common people*', or the possibility that they may, one day, be loaded with cash, which, somehow, will take away all the angst they and their peers suffer on a daily basis. It's funny, we are all told in the UK that there is no class system any longer, which may be true to a certain extent. However, as someone from a working-class upbringing, I do have what could be described as a 'chip on my shoulder'. This 'chip' makes me default to anything remotely working class and despise anything I consider to be 'middle class', the people who, through what I consider to be my upbringing, I despise. There is, however, a line from a song written by a working-class icon, which has troubled me from my early teenage years. A line, which has given me the impression that some kind of conspiracy is at work, especially as the man that penned it was shot dead in the street – sometime after its inception. The song in question was written by John Lennon and it was entitled *'Working Class Hero'*. John Lennon, as portrayed by the media, was the archetypal working-class hero, having come from humble beginnings in Liverpool to super stardom. It is fair to say, he and his scouse mates were, and probably still are, inspirational to working-class people worldwide. As stated above, I have a working-class 'chip' on my shoulders and just like my piers I am proud to call myself working class. My confusion in this context derives from the lines, 'A working class hero is something to be, you are all fucking peasants, as far as I can see.'

# ASK YOURSELF WHY?

It's quite clear that the so-called 'developed' countries of the world are suffering from an 'obesity crisis'. We hear almost every day that our lives are at risk due to the ever-increasing side effects of carrying too much fat. We are told that the next generation is going to die way before it is supposed to do, leaving us 'middle agers' to fend for ourselves.

I have asked myself many times during my lifetime, am I vastly overweight, or am I pandering to the media's obsession with making us paranoid? Firstly, and this is probably important for you to note, I am not a dietician, a doctor, or an expert in all matters of nutrition. I am a regular 'middle-aged bloke' who, at two different stages of my life decided that I needed to lose weight. Both times I managed to lose a considerable amount (up to six stones). However, the first weight loss event was followed by 20 years of gradual weight gain, taking me to the point where the dial on my bathroom scales was exceeded. A point of note from my experience is, however, whenever I look at myself in the mirror, regardless of weight or age, I always look the same!

This fact alone dissuaded me from considering any further attempts to lose weight. After all, you only live once, why not enjoy every minute of it?

The writing of this book has taken place over a period of years and having revisited many times, I have decided to slot this paragraph into the text, as it, through my own experience has become an important part of my thinking. This ever so important element of the whole weight issue, is the ability to maintain your desired weight. How often have you heard people complain that having been on a diet and having lost vast amounts of weight, they have managed to regain it all and some more? It has become clear to me, not because I consider myself an expert, but because of my own experience, that there are certain types of people, who, through eating certain types and quantities of food, will gain weight very easily. We have all seen those who purport to have the ability to eat exactly what they want, when they want, with not a sign of any weight gain, or others who have the problem of actually putting weight on.

It is important to note that, like anything else in life, the whole weight loss issue is a lottery, played by people with innumerable differences in terms of their body and mind functions, with an unfathomable amount of differences in taste, lifestyles, in fact almost everything. I suppose what I am trying to say is that no two people are the same and although the world's most eminent experts concoct theories about what we should and shouldn't be eating, they couldn't possibly begin to base their theories on every human being on the planet.

What is clear is that in the UK, some people appear to be eating themselves to death. As a person who has a certain amount of obsession with fatties, I find myself quite often people-watching. In the past, I have spent hours waiting for flights and trains taking account of people who, are not just overweight, but who seem to be defying the laws of gravity with their ability to elevate the large quantities of blubber!

In my lifetime I have seen the amount of 'really fat' people, spread from America, across the 'pond' to the UK. America, for example, still manages to surprise me, in that the 'norm' in terms of the general appearance of people portrayed in the media, appears to be getting larger and fatter, with the fattest people being generally poor and female. (However, males don't fare much better.) My main observation point at present is the exit stream at my local supermarket. It sounds a bit weird, but, at the end of our weekly shop, I am banished from the checkout area by my better half, due to my incompetence at packing bags and consistent impatience. This sees me banished to the waiting area which, as you will appreciate, gives a nutter like me the opportunity to conduct my studies. As a constant stream of people enter and leave the store, many appear to be overweight. However, with what seems to be increasing frequency, many are 'jaw-droppingly' overweight. Years ago and basing my early life experiences in Oldham in Lancashire, I imagine that some of the people I observe would have stopped the traffic in say 1973. However, in 2016 they are becoming more and more the norm.

I will talk later about the media and creative industries and how the norm is, to a certain extent, created by them. We are constantly blasted with images which, it is apparent, give the likes of you and me a perception of how we should look. Statisticians, when analysing 'stuff', may refer to the ultimate 'norm' as the median line, which in terms of the fatty issue could be described as the ultimate way to appear. However, even statisticians understand that not everything can be perfect all the time, so they allow tolerances, such as in our case, allowing a permissible skinny or fat deviation to 'perfection'. This is referred to as the standard deviation which, when trying to maintain the quality of a manufactured product, is a good guide as to what should be rejected, however, and this is only the theory. This standard deviation appears to affect our judgement of what is an acceptable appearance. The cynic in me, particularly when it comes to big fashion products, suspects a conspiracy at work, given that the fashion industry is shop fronted through magazines and increasingly online. Take a company making jeans, for example, and let's for the purpose of the exercise look at a global brand. Regardless of how desirable the garments produced by that company are, as far as the company is concerned, the more desirable their brand, the more units they are going to sell. They certainly do not give a flying fuck whether their jeans will get you laid! Their whole modus operandi is to maximise profits and more units equals more profit. Now the company, if they are going to deliver big returns, needs to look at the cost of sourcing the materials and manufacturing the goods. It is well known and accepted, especially having been brought up in the cotton capital of the UK, that the cost of labour is too great on this island and we all know that our high street fashion items are made in areas where the costs of labour week on week are less than some people in the West spend on dog food. So, if these companies can get labour costs down to a pittance and I'm sure they drive a pretty hard bargain when it comes to sourcing materials, where do they go to make even more profit? My guess is by the amount of material they use in each unit they produce. Take jeans for example, I am not a maths genius, but I would hazard a guess that the material utilised to make a 30-inch waist pair of jeans is less than that used to make a size 40-inch waist equivalent. Multiply this simple equivalent by tens of thousands of pairs of jeans and you don't need to be a Nobel Prize winning physicist to deduct that it is better for profits if you can knock out more of the smaller size. Of course, this obvious business decision would never be screamed from the rooftops by some of the global brands. However, I'm more than convinced that board meetings around the world must have toiled with this, particularly during the current increase in the number of fatties around the place. Given this cynical business model, it is a stroll in the park to look to the high fashion media, who too need to maximise their profits, by charging stupid amounts per magazine, or subscription and by becoming desirable as a shop front for the manufacturer of the jeans, which obviously comes down to the size of the readership. Fashion, along with the art world and even the world of the wine snobs, in my humble opinion does not follow any kind of logic. In economics there is a theory known as 'product elasticity' which determines how well a product will sell according to its price. To the casual observer this would indicate that the cheaper a product is, particularly a desirable product, the more units it will sell. Our current state of flux in the West has turned this on its head, with the current thinking in clothing, art and even burgers being, the more expensive the product, the more desirable it becomes and ergo the more units it will sell. Noam Chomsky, one of my modern day heroes, has, in my opinion, hit the nail right on the head with his theory on 'just enough'. I am probably misrepresenting here. However, I'll try to elaborate.

The fashion industry puts on a big show, with so-called super models draped in clothing designed by our greatest creatives. The show is strewn with the whole circus of actors, musicians, sports' personalities, the media and all the other bullshit which is so important to these 'types', giving a sense that looking at a few dresses is a really important issue. One of the musicians endorses a particular piece of cloth by paying an eye-watering amount for it and is seen wearing it at one of those awards ceremonies. You know, those events where the entertainment pricks jerk each other off about how brilliant they are. So, we now have a piece of cloth, worn by a skeletal icon, designed by one of the in-vogue designers, with a price tag way outside of your spray tanning, gym-going biscuit factory worker. How does this pleb get to wear the brand or look anything like Skeletor? Well, you might not be able to afford the dress, but how about wearing a pair of sunglasses with the brand's logo stamped on the side? They only cost a fraction of a penny to make, as they were made in Bangladesh by a three-year-old, but you could get a piece of the action for ... shall we say, £250.00? Sold! Just wait while the custard cream crew get a look at these 'bad-boys', they'll be green with envy, and perhaps they might think that I look like Skeletor, or even better, strangers might actually think I'm her! (Now I'm just being silly, I think it's time I moved on.)

As time goes by, we are bombarded with differing opinions by 'so-called' experts, who advise on what we should and should not be eating. Fat, for example, is sometimes good, sometimes bad, saturated, unsaturated and comes in all different shapes and forms, so I am told. So, what then am I supposed to do, eat it or not? It is clear that given two or three days with little or no food, it is quite possible I would consider eating my own shoes and the eminent advice being doled out daily would not even factor into my decision-making process

The reasons for me originally losing weight were numerous, and were based on my 'time of life'. As I indicated earlier, I had two weight loss events, the first aged 19-20 the second aged 50-52. However, in summary, the following are the main drivers which kick started my desire to 'slim down':

### *To be more attractive to the opposite sex*

A famous psychological theorist by the name of Abraham Maslow developed what is famously known as the 'Hierarchy of Needs Theory'. The theory describes, by use of a pyramid diagram, the issues that drive human beings throughout their lives. The bottom of the pyramid, known as the physiological section, describes the absolute base requirements, the issues that, if not accounted for, will not allow a person to move up the pyramid to experience issues of a 'higher nature' or be able to live at all. Amongst those base issues is 'sex'. We have been, and continue to be, told that not being fat will bag you a mate. Note, I say 'not being fat' as opposed to saying 'being thin', as there is a point where we are told that being thin is counterproductive to your potential for sex. It is worth noting that in the past in our culture and even today in others, being fat is a good thing when putting you 'out there'. The actual nirvana for the Western male could be best illustrated by the famous office scene advertisement. There are many different versions, all of which convey the same, basic message: A group of reasonably successful, empowered female office workers find themselves ogling an Adonis, who happens to be mowing a lawn or cleaning an office window. The women, who due to their success and a desire to live life to the full, devise ingenious ways to have a 'look' at what the Adonis is 'packing'. In all cases they use the product being advertised, as quite clearly the product not only leads to success and security, it also is so desirable and refreshing that the Adonis has no choice but to open the can to consume it. Hilariously, on opening the can, the contents spray the Adonis, giving him the opportunity to remove his shirt. The vision portrayed to the empowered female office workers is a site to behold, to the extent that they are dumbstruck with lust. However, this lust only lasts for a few seconds, as the Adonis continues with his labours and the women return to being empowered and successful. Another attribute to this scene, is that amongst the empowered female office workers there is not one 'fatty'. The messages I'm getting from this are:

- Fatties don't belong in this scene (nor do skinnies for that matter).
- Drinking this concoction of chemicals and gas is maybe the very product that will get you, if not laid, at least the admiration of your 'good looking' peers.

Interestingly enough, in my half a century plus on the planet, I have seen a marked change in the way in which the arts and media wankers inform us on how the sexes are supposed to behave. As someone who watches quite a lot of free UK television, I am constantly bombarded by adverts, trying to convince mainly women, that they need to look younger or climb mountains while menstruating, or intense dramas, or soaps where, on the whole, the women, particularly middle-aged women, seem to be obsessed with 'cock'. The proliferation of old women ogling young men's 'bum-cakes' seems to be occurring increasingly, which, as someone of a certain age, I can relate back a few years to when it was men who partook of this practice. This transformation of 'dirty old men' to 'dirty old women' is from my perception, due in part to our cultural need to conform and consume. Conforming, from the perspective of behaving like you perceive you should. This begs the question 'how do you gain your perceptions?' Well, you don't need to be very clever to work that one out!

I'll probably 'bang on' about it again at some point, but I'm very interested about what I understand to be the 'CIA's slide response theory'. Not wanting to get into too much detail, the theory works on the basis that, if a group of people are subjected to a certain stimulus for a certain amount of time, they will, because of the way in which the brain is 'hard-wired', dismiss or accept certain information given to them immediately, without questioning the facts. Examples of this may include:

- Muslims are terrorists.
- Global warming is your fault.
- Homosexuality. I'll leave you to debate that subject.
- Wars do more harm to children than any others. This is quite interesting. Up until only a few years ago, this statement would have named women and children. However, women seem to have dropped out of the equation for some reason.

It has just occurred to me; it may appear to the reader that I am having a 'pop' at women, which, as anyone's slide response reaction would be to brandish me as a 'misogynist'. Or my comments above regarding homosexuals and Muslims would tarnish me with the title of 'homophobe' or 'Islamaphobe'. Please, if you are going to continue to read on, get this straight. I have no compunction to chastise any group of people for where they stick their dicks, or indeed how they prey to their God. I do, however, take umbrage with groups that, using the slide response, pigeonhole me into one or more of the 'ists' – sexist, racist, etc. It's amazing; the 'holier than thou' politically correct pricks, by tagging people with an 'ist' first, then feel free to bestow further vitriol.

I had this issue myself recently, whereby a mediocre painter, by associating me with the term 'bully' (we should all stand up against bullying!), went on in a correspondence to someone else to use this as a justification to assassinate my character and to further justify the reasons for the dickish behaviour, displayed by this particular person.

Fatties (I'm going to concentrate on them from now on, as this is what the book is about) in the office women's scenario above are excluded and to the hormone-driven 19-year-old, the message is clear. 'If you want to get any kind of action with anybody remotely as attractive as these people, you need to lose weight, and in order to do that, you need to drink our product. It is noteworthy that the stereotypes used in this particular advert are working class, as once you move up the financial ladder, as a fatty, you have more than a 'six-pack' in your armoury of attractiveness. Money being possibly the main weapon, in the greed-ridden world that we aspire to.

Adverts such as this, coupled with extraordinary brand triggers, such as billboard adverts, magazines and product placements, make it impossible for the fatty to escape the inevitable conclusion: 'You are fat, you don't belong and you need to do something about it.' The message, when considering I am referring to one product, is absolutely overwhelming when you consider the plethora of brands conveying the same message. As a 19-year-old, it is easy to see the drivers to lose weight developed from feelings of self-loathing and not belonging become untenable, and in a number of cases boost the sales of canned chemicals to an increasing number of paranoid individuals. As a 50-year-old, however, it is perceived that you have drank enough of that shite to realise how shallow the whole carbonated drink message actually is. Which, funnily enough, is probably why the advertisement referred to above excludes anyone over their mid-thirties.

In summary, an overwhelming reason for a fatty, particularly a young fatty to lose weight is in order to attract a mate of the best possible calibre. I'm sure there are numerous biological and base instinctual drivers behind this, but I'll leave that discussion for somebody who knows what they are talking about. It is also worth noting at this stage that my sexual orientation is 'heterosexual' and my perceptions and aspirations are based on this premise. Not wanting to sound like an out-and-out homophobe however, I am not familiar with the triggers attracting same sex mates, so if I am discounting the 'gay view', it is due to my lack of knowledge and not prejudice.

***Clothing***

It was said, famously, by Mark Twain: 'Clothes make the man. Naked people have little or no influence on society.' That's quite an interesting point. Just as above, our self- perception of what to wear is imposed upon us based on what we think we want to emit. There is the, in the words of ZZ Top, *'every girl's crazy about the sharp dressed man'* or as in the famous denim scenario, the Adonis, stripping down to his boxer shorts in the launderette. The object of desire in this particular instance is a pair of jeans, which, although made of canvas, like, I think it is safe to say all other jeans, are so effective at making you look like an Adonis, they will cost you three times the price of your 'bog-standard' pair. As a self-confessed fatty, I have tried in the past, to purchase a pair of these 'miracle pants' but have been left in despair as, in most shops in the UK, a 36-inch waist is the largest size on sale (38 at a push). I have, however, in a bid to 'belong', managed to purchase these objects of 'desire' from the USA. However, even with them on, there is still a big problem for the fatty. I first encountered this problem, aged nine. As a working-class boy from the Lancashire town of Oldham, my peers were all wearing this brand of denim, matched with cherry-red boots and Crombie coats, with a Lancashire rose emblazoned on the chest pocket. I desired all these things immensely. After weeks, or more likely months of consistent harassment from me, my parents finally admitted defeat and took me to 'The Famous Army & Navy Stores' to get my first pair of this particular brand of jeans. I was paraplegic with excitement. It is at this point in my life, as a nine-year old, that I first became aware that I was a fatty. Aged nine, my weight was nine stones and for the next few years, up to the age of 18, my weight in stones almost exactly mirrored my age in years. However, back to the nine-year-old. The jeans in question (I'm sure that you are aware of the brand by now) have a leather patch on the back, with the company logo emblazoned on it (a good thing). However, much to the utter dismay of a nine-year-old fatty, the patch also contains statistical information, most notably, the waist size! Mine, at this stage in life, was 32 inches; up to four inches greater than my peers. Plus the back pockets, which in themselves are a brand icon, were, it seemed, infinitely bigger that the pockets sewn onto the jeans of my peers. After initial 'comments' of a derogatory nature, the issue dissipated and as any nine-year-old of the time, I 'just got on with it'. However, it is around this time that the label 'fatty' came into my day-to-day life.

Moving on in childhood, into the life as a teenager, I was fraught with anxiety every time I went to buy clothes, basically because my school uniform and 'going out clothes' were bought from shops catering for fully grown men. As a fashion indoctrinated teenager, my clothes never seemed to match up to the level of fashion as those of my peers (spoilt bastards). On leaving school, the problem escalated as now I found that, in a World of buying my own clothes, the shops offered little above a 38 waist, or a 50-inch chest. This is what prompted my first successful weight loss event. I am keen to point out at this stage, that I am loath to use the word diet for the following reasons:

- As a fatty, losing weight, in my experience, is not about 'a diet', on the contrary, as I write, correcting the text following sterling work by the Amender, I am mindful of yet another media ploy to make us think that we are helpless. It's like this, a programme entitled, something along the lines of 'Obesity, you are fucked,' is given prime time television space, The programme is fronted by , let's be brutal here, a glamorous 'thicky' Now do not get me wrong here, I'm sure that the presenter is very successful in their World, however, it is plain to see that they are the link between us common, thick people and the 'experts,' you know, those who get to wear the lab coats and convince us that they know best. Recently, while watching a prime time programme of this nature, I was amazed to discover that the answer to every fatty's woes could be summarised by, wait for it, a behavioural economist! What the fuck! A bit later in the programme, some lab coat wearing academic displayed a computer application, which, flashed pictures of broccoli in front of the user, which, as was explained to us thick people trained the subconscious mind into eating healthily, leading to, you guessed it, weight loss. To prove this as being fact, they used the app on volunteers, who, after a month of this bullshit managed to lose 1 kilogramme in weight! I can lose 1 kilogram, as can you, in 30 seconds, just by taking a shit!

- Being a fatty is somewhat akin to being an alcoholic or a drug addict and that the cure for all of the above comes from more than abstinence alone.
- Diet, in my view, indicates some sort of 'fad' which, in my experience come and go. It is noteworthy that some of the diet books are produced by persons with vast knowledge of all manner of dietary expertise. Some

however, are celebrity endorsements, and as can be seen 'celebrity sells'! On the dietary expertise subject, I recently discussed my intention to write this book with a few close friends, and although the feedback was positive, the message that I would need scientific proof and being open to litigation came forward time and time again. Let's be clear at this point, I am not a scientist, I am not a celebrity, I have however, on two occasions taken steps to reduce my weight to a level at which I am happy. The intention of this book is to inform 'like-minded' people of what worked for me and leave the detail to the individuals concerned. Our culture, at the time of writing, is to be 'spoon fed' every step of the way and if it doesn't work, 'it's somebody else's fault' (where there's blame there's a claim).

During my first weight loss event, I reduced my weight, over the period of 18 months from 18 ½ stones to 12 ½ stones. This reduced my statistics from waist 40 to waist 32 and my chest from 52 to 42. Part way during this event, I remember vividly going to the new boutique, which had opened by the 'Iron railings' in Oldham Town Centre and getting myself a pair of mustard-coloured jumbo cords … 36-inch waist! I had arrived!

In more recent years, my need to belong through the medium of clothing, has been less motivated by the need to look good in the disco, but moreover, to be able to purchase off-the-peg clothes at high street prices. I, for various reasons such as weddings, job interviews and the like, find the need, on occasion, to wear a suit. Over the years, once purchased, a suit would be worn possibly ten times over a ten year period. The older, more financially astute person I have developed into, pragmatically understands that the need for me to be seen perusing the buffets of weddings in an expensive suit is frivolous to say the least. Therefore, an off-the-peg '50 quid number' would fit the bill perfectly. With this in mind and moving this tale of woe from Oldham to Aberystwyth, I took to frequenting a famous high street clothing discount store, you know the one that sells t-shirts which align the wearer to surf shack in Huntington Beach, CA., even though the wearer has never been further than Magaluf!

To my dismay, I had crept out of the size range once more, with a 52-inch chest and a 42-inch waist. My only option, in an Aberystwyth context, was to visit a 'gentlemen's' outfitters, where via some level of embarrassment, due to the sales assistant having to go to the back room to dig out a 'fatty suit', I would leave with a very fine, very expensive (five times the cost) set of clothes. On a more casual note, I latched onto an elderly couple, who, twice a year, went to Las Vegas. On their return, I would dash round to their house and pick up two pairs of branded jeans, which, as you will appreciate coming from the US, fitted my ample arse to perfection. However, this started to become unsustainable, as the elderly couple's route came to an end, and my wardrobe became full of expensive clothes that I never wore. At this stage in my life I became aware of another phenomenon that would eventually lead to my second weight loss event - the advent of social media.

I suppose it is vanity driving me to wanting to 'conform' and wear clothing that I perceive will be acceptable to others and I believe it to be vanity that the clothing industry, particularly at the 'top end' of the market, use to cream those at the lower end of the financial spectrum. I recently spent many hours hanging around airport departure lounges, going to and from work on a weekly commute. During a particular assignment I spent hours in Munich airport, and, to help pass the time spent hours looking at 'things' which, let's face it, are things that you would want, rather than need, notwithstanding emergency purchases, say from the pharmacy.

**Note:** The 'want-need' theory is, in my opinion, important not only as a mantra for losing weight, but should be applied to almost every potential purchase by those, who like so many, live on a budget. For those not familiar with the theory, you should ask the question do I 'WANT' this or do I 'NEED' it? WANT, loosely termed is 'a desire for something', whereas NEED is to require (something) because it is essential or very important rather than just desirable.

So, if you were to apply this theory to say a pair of designer sunglasses, which were displayed alongside a cheaper pair, I think you can guess where this is going. However, we are talking about the consumption of food and weight loss. Moreover, we are talking about it from the perspective of a society, which, throughout my whole life, has had the ability to source untold amounts of food at the 'drop of a hat'. What if this was not the case? What if all the supermarkets and food suppliers, due to a bad harvest or a war, for example, had nothing. It is clear that very quickly, food would become a 'NEED' item as opposed to a 'WANT'. The point being, if you do not eat, you will die. This last statement may be the subject of debate by those who use liquidisers to produce green detox slop. However, just to shut you fuckers up, my scenario will shut all the power stations down, so you will need to mush your shit manually!

Ask the question: 'Why do I eat?' As a power station requires gas or coal to power its turbines and generate energy, so we **need** fuel – in the form of food – to power our continued existence (screen grabbed from Google). So, we are taking on board fuel to exist just like the driver who visits the fuel station when the tank drops to a certain level. Fatties, it is clear, take on too much fuel and are able to store it in the form of fat. Unfortunately vehicles only have a finite storage capacity, which stops drivers stopping at every filling station to take on more fuel, or to remain in the same station taking on more fuel than their tank can hold.

On one particular occasion, during a period of time spent in an airport departure lounge, I decided I would get something for my boys, who at the time, like most youngsters, were keen on 'designer' clothing. I searched through the designer shops, looking at jackets that cost £2,000.00 pounds (no chance!) and various other ridiculously priced unnecessary items. Eventually I spied some plain t-shirts made by a company that even I recognised. To my dismay, they cost £135.00 each!

Needless to say, they didn't make it into my bag! A couple of weeks later, I watched a very interesting documentary which illustrated how companies that are producing 'luxury' items use the 'just enough' approach, resulting in them making vast amounts of revenue selling 'cheap shit' to the poor by producing expensive shit to adorn the wealthy, or foolish, creating a long line 'envy chain' based on vanity and aspiration. So, a film star is at the premier of his latest film (I'll use a bloke in this instance, but women are just the same). It is not uncommon for designer clothing manufacturers to loan or even give him a suit to appear in. Often the 'brand' of suit is leaked, usually by the trash media from which we glean most of our false aspirations. Looking objectively at a suit, one looks pretty much the same as the next, when seen through the lens of a camera, be it a £65.00 discount store job, or a £10,000.00 bespoke or designer number. However, the £10,000.00 suit is worn by film stars who can afford them. Those who can't afford them, let's face it are 'losers'. Very cleverly, the 'labels' then produce cheaper branded items such as t-shirts, jeans, shoes and even sunglasses. Again, these items on the face of it, look just the same as cheaper shit, with the exceptions being the brand label, which is available for display and the price tag which, as you travel up and down the envy chain, is always seen as expensive to some of those who aspire to play the game. It was interesting that during recent civil unrest in the UK, the poorer elements of society were involved in a massive urban looting spree. Their objects of desire were 'stuff', not food (although I'm sure some was stolen) but designer sportswear, televisions and things you would want rather than need. The envy chain, in my opinion, was seen here in its most basic form as it is apparent that younger people in society, be them fatties or otherwise, feel that they need to belong to 'the tribe', and to belong you must consume the correct stuff.

This is borne out by instances such as:

- There are numerous scare-mongering documentaries on television studying UK gang culture. The gang members, who it seems have easy access to automatic weapons, almost without exception blame their lifestyle on poverty and their feelings of helplessness. The rewards for their excessive risk taking are without question, large wads of cash, expensive cars and designer clothing and accessories. All of which, as can be seen on the programme are photographed, usually alongside bottles of champagne. Their 'pay-day' if you like, is that they can raise the perception that they live the lives of the film stars and those who can legitimately afford the shallow existence of the rich and famous often portrayed by our trash media.

- Being born and bred in the Lancashire mill town of Oldham, I was, from a young age, very much aware that Oldham lived very much in the shadow of Manchester (their town centres are probably less than ten miles apart). Football has, during my lifetime, always been a large part of the culture in the North West of England. Myself, I have since 1973, been a supporter of Oldham Athletic, with them being my local team it makes perfect sense. This, however, was not the case for a large number of my peers. They chose to support Manchester United, who obviously are a much larger tribe and affiliation with them gives the supporter the perception of being successful. This, in my opinion, gave the clothing manufacturers a gold-plated opportunity to cream the poorer parts of society, by mass-producing stuff, such as football shirts, at a fraction of pennies per unit and selling them to those who want to belong at thousands of percent 'mark-up'. Again, the envy chain is utilised to the maximum.

What, you may ask, has all this got to do with me wanting to lose weight? I suppose the point I am trying to make, is that clothing and the need to belong to a tribe, or impress your peers, is, in my opinion, a 'shallow' reason to lose weight. People come in a vast number of shapes and sizes and some of them are picked up by the creative industries to sell shit to the masses. I am not personally in a position, from a financial perspective, where I can have all my clothes made for me. My issue was being able to go to the nearest shop and get something to wear, without the rigmarole of having to search for and never finding exactly what I need at the time of asking

You may recall in one of my opening paragraphs I indicated that, in the mirror, I always look the same? This is not true when I look at a photograph of myself. In a photograph, my age and in particular my fatty appearance, is as plain as day. Being involved in social media gave me access to numerous photographic representations of myself in full colour, giving rise to the inevitable conclusion that I must lose weight.

### *Health*

This aspect of being a fatty is one in which the 'experts' leave me for 'dead' (excuse the pun). It seems that the negative health effects of being a fatty are undoubtedly well known. Diabetes, heart trouble, bone and joint disorders, the list is endless. A point of particular interest that I have noted with regards the scientific community's information regarding weight and health is that it is almost unanimous that poor, working-class, people are more likely to be obese than those of a more affluent disposition. I recently spent a few months working in Greater Manchester and was lucky enough to be located near to an area known as Partington. I don't for one minute pretend to know the socio-economic make-up of the population of this area, however, I was lucky enough to, on occasion, leave my workplace and drive down to the local shopping area in my lunch hour to pick up something for lunch. The area in question, which to be fair was in a state of disrepair and neglect, comprised a bank, a baker, a chip shop, a bookies, a paper shop and a co-op supermarket (the latter being in a reasonable state of repair). The area reminded me of the 1970s utopian, community architecture, with a shopping hub, surrounded by a mass of affordable housing, and although seemingly run-down, remained vibrant and lively. The key words which best describe, from my perspective, the outsider's perception of the area are as follows:

- Pies
- Fags (or cigarettes if you are not from the UK!)
- Tattoos (mainly on women)

- National Lottery
- Unemployment
- Fat

On the final point, when I say fat, I mean 'FAT'. In some instances, I found myself drawn into staring in awe and questioning how some people could dress themselves, indeed where they could find the clothes to dress themselves in! Some of those amongst a seemingly endless stream of obese people must have been struggling to walk or even breathe. What was clear, however, is it seems that they did not have similar problems when it came to eating or amassing fat about their person.

A question that occurred to me was, do those people, who surely have problems negotiating their rear ends around corners, see themselves as 'non-fatty' when they look in the mirror? Surely if they could see themselves as I do they would do something about it? It must be said, however, that confidence levels seemed pretty high, and the media portrayal of self-loathing of fatties was by no means evident, as people went about their day-to-day business much like any other public space on the planet.

I implore anyone to sit in any town centre shopping area for half an hour. It would be best to sit outside a high street clothing retailer, as it is likely you will witness a lot of 'foot-traffic'. While sitting there, try the following if you are looking for proof that the 'fatty nightmare' is more than prevalent in today's society, keep your eyes peeled for someone who you consider to be morbidly obese. On spotting, keep an eye on them until they have passed. On their passing, widen your observation for the next subject of your attention. I'll guarantee that if you cannot see another subject immediately, you will, within 30 seconds.

When my kids were younger, we were lucky enough to spend holidays in California and I remember seeing people who made my jaw drop due to the extent of their obesity and remember being aware of the fact that it seemed to be the norm, as people passed each other without a second glance. In 1970s Oldham, these people, if seen outside of a circus, would have stopped traffic!

I could 'harp on' about the negative health impacts associated with being a fatty for chapters. However, as it is very well documented, I think it's probably best to leave it there.

**General Appearance**

You only have to watch television, read a paper or magazine, or look at the billboards to decipher the required societal requirements regarding appearance. The pressure, it seems, to 'look a certain way' is heaped on women. However, with the ever-increasing emergence of the 'man-bag', moobs and the need for men to moisturise, it won't be long before the mantra 'because you're worth it' emanates through the perception of every 'metro-sexual'. The peer pressure to conform, in terms of appearance seems to hold no bounds, in particular with youngsters. The cultural shift in terms of '60 is the new 30' has netted a whole new section of consumers who would do anything to conform.

Putting fatties to one side for a moment, I have a number of burning questions regarding the bastards who sell us shite to smell and look good, while remaining adequately moisturised:

*My understanding regarding the mechanics of soap, is that it works by breaking down the oils in your skin, which carry the dirt which you want to remove. In some cases, the removal of such oils results in dry skin. In order to remedy the dry skin problem, there are a number of products available which, not only replace lost oils, but magically make the user look younger resulting in members of the opposite sex being involved in vehicular accidents, as their concentration is overtaken by overwhelming beauty. That taken into account, and unless you really need to degrease your skin, for example if you are a coal miner, why bother? Would not water alone do 'the trick'?*

*At the time of writing, the religious garb of female Muslims is a hot topic, in that, as a society we are not sure whether we like it or not, mainly as it obscures the actual appearance of the person contained within a wrap of black cloth. It is seen to some as a disguise, used to infiltrate the infidel masses, prior to blowing them up. (Why do they bother? The repeated excuse for such anti-social behaviour is 'modesty'. Really? Are you so modest that you cannot let anybody see you?)*

*There is hardly a woman, and increasingly so a man, who would not leave the house without applying make-up. In some cases, the 'slap' application is so extensive, the clown-like appearance almost completely masks the actual appearance of the wearer. Is that not, too, a disguise? I'm sure there are numbers of women who wear absolutely no make - up at all, who at this stage are nodding in agreement, as they shoe another stallion, but the point I am making is that to a certain extent, the very nature of a person's cultural appearance is to disguise what you actually look like and appear as close as possible to the cultural norms that are rammed down your throat from the second you emerge from your pit. The companies putting out the message 'you're worth it' understand that your vanity and desire for a feeling of belonging is so great that you would, if told, smear dog shit on your face and pay a fucking fortune for the pleasure of doing so!*

From a fatty's perspective, appearance is dealt with in a number of ways; the most infuriating of which is the 'I'm happy being a larger person'. This, in all but the most exceptional of cases, is an out-and-out lie. I guess in medieval times when being a fatty was seen as a route to affluence, the dismissal of the 'happy to be fat' would be open to challenge. However, in today's 'you're worth it' society, being a fatty is not a good thing and we are reminded of this almost every hour of our waking lives, by the media, our peers and when we go shopping for clothes. In these days of out-and-out individualism, save for those of us who make all our own clothes, we are confined to the sizes stocked in the clothing outlets. In years gone by, attendance at a music festival, for example, was seen as a way of escaping completely the rigours of day-to-day grinding misery and, to some, an opportunity to express themselves outside of the 'norm'. Appearance did not matter, in fact come to think of it, neither did clothing! It was quite acceptable to get completely bollock naked and following a visit to the 'smack and black' tent, get up to the front of the pyramid stage and partake in mental hippy dancing while quenching your thirst with rough cider (£1 a gallon from the Lancashire hippy tent). Nowadays, even such bastions of freedom have been overtaken as the mainstream media take themselves en masse, to every festival possible. It was a sad day for the fatty when a scrawny model appeared on the front of all the garbage press papers in a flowery dress and a pair of £3,000 wellies. The following season, we were entreated to 'get the festival look this season'! Since then, I have noticed that festivals, particularly Glasto, have become a rite of passage for middle class, white, spoilt, post university, or, even worse, gap year youngsters, who, take great care to achieve the 'festival look' as it would be sacrilege to appear 'out of context' on your Facebook profile.

Fatties, therefore, are forced into convention, by the fact that if they are unable to buy clothing in the sizes that fit them, their freedom to express themselves in whatever way they require, is governed by the clothing that is available to them. I often wonder whether this fact has given rise to 'fat goths'.

That having been said, and partly I am convinced due to the number of fatties, the advertising media have started to appeal to their perceived mass market. One particular advert, aimed at women from size 12 to circus tent, displays two deliriously happy women, the slimmer one pouting and loving the camera, quickly followed by the fat fucker dancing about her daily business in garish shite. Both are very, very happy and the fatty in particular is so happy that she's found some shit to wear that she has resorted to dancing. My immediate thoughts on this is that the fatty couldn't possibly do that much dancing, otherwise she wouldn't be so fat, unless of course she spends most of her time dancing to the local chip shop.

# WHAT ARE YOU GOING TO DO ABOUT IT?

At the time of writing, the Don Henley song '*In a New York Minute*' is playing on the DAB radio in my kitchen. The point being, in the period of time being referred to, the song goes on to tell the listener that 'everything can change'. If you want to lose weight you have to be committed to the cause, giving up at any point will not yield the results you need and probably lead to your self-loathing in the future. Therefore, there is a beginning to your being the weight that you require, so it is important that you have a start date.

All that having been said, it is of vast importance, during what I consider to be a lifestyle change, to never 'beat yourself up' if you are lured in by a day, week or month of 'straying' from your plan, as long as you can keep clear in your mind that you have strayed and that it's not the end of the world. Again, I need to emphasise that I am not a doctor or eminent dietician; I am a normal bloke who has lost some weight and, at the time of writing, have managed to maintain the weight that I am happy with for roughly three years. During that time and based on my perceptions derived from the many sources of information available, it has become clear to me that the mind has a serious role to play in your achieving your ultimate goal. However, my day-to-day eating habits have adopted what I consider to be 'the least path of resistance' theory to control how my body deals with what I put into it.

The analogy behind the theory is somewhat akin to a stream, which, while winding its way to wherever it is going, will take the easiest route available to it. If part of a water-course is dammed (not in the biblical sense), the stream will eventually find an easier route to run, which may of course be over the dam itself. Adapting this theory to food consumption and purely from a layman's viewpoint, I look at carbs, such as bread, rice and potatoes as 'easy' in that given the choice, your body will devour these first, probably as they are easiest to digest (not sure on that one). Proteins, however, I deal with as 'hard', taking longer to break down (and possibly consuming more calories during the digestive process). If you look at your average Western style meal, the balanced approach will result in a mixture of 'easy' and 'hard'. Your body, when faced with the job of digesting will start with the easy, putting the hard to one side before involving itself in the 'hard graft'. During this process, and it is highly likely to be the case with a fatty, another 'full load' is taken on board before the 'hard' has been fully digested. This leaves the system with a dilemma: get on and finish the hard or store what's left of the hard as fat and get into the easy stuff contained in the next consignment. What if, the theory asks, you were to cut down or cut out the 'easy' and make your body work on the 'hard'? My asking this question has certainly yielded the results I need. I can hear all the experts shouting from the rooftops that this theory falls down on numerous levels for so many reasons and as I said, I'm no expert, but I have lost the weight I wanted, have improved my health and stamina and in general laugh at your scientific theories as they are dismissed by the next bullshit scientific theories, which are usually driven by food manufacturers wanting to sell the latest crap they are bringing to market.

On the subject of protein, my conspiracy radar is on 'full alert', particularly when it comes to the massive consumption of protein shite, such as whey protein. Let me explain my theory starting with milk. When I was a child, we had our milk delivered to the door by the farmer, who milked the cows, cooled the milk in a tank, bottled it and delivered it daily. Then it seemed, during the 1970s that, possibly due to TB or similar nasties, it was decided all milk needed to be pasteurised or sterilised to protect the public. Small farmers, not having the money or space and using the 'least path of resistance' started to sell their produce via tankers into cooperatives and to what have since become gigantic operations. Over the years, due to the offshoot of industries such as cheese production, as an example, these organisations must have found themselves overflowing with increasing amounts of whey. This, if I am correct, used to get sold into animal feed markets, which notably is a product with all 'the good stuff' taken out of it and a waste product. Scroll on a few years down the line and this waste product is repackaged, marketed to the 'bewildered herds' (Chomsky again) and is now an expensive 'essential' to the gym-going lemmings. What a fantastic business model; it is somewhat akin to the famous quote from Marie-Antoinette (bride of France's King Louis XVI) who, when told that her subjects had no bread to eat, was heard to shout 'let them eat cake', this being a much cheaper alternative. Imagine, if the quote had been 'fuck em', let them eat/drink pig swill, oh, and incidentally make sure it costs the stupid bastards a fortune and I get some of the profits'. I would imagine the peasants' revolt may have happened a bit quicker!

A common excuse for not committing to a weight reduction lifestyle is that doing so does not fit in to the 'busy life' of today's modern person. This is perpetuated by the supermarkets who mass produce ready meals, branded with all the right signals to lure fatties in, in their desperation to lose weight without doing a thing. Sure, three minutes in a microwave for a delicious, exotic meal fits the bill perfectly. However, the salt, sugar and chemical concoctions included in these exotic dishes can't be good for you (as the branding would suggest). The supermarkets must be rubbing their hands with glee at the gargantuan profits made from mass-producing slop at fractions of a penny per portion and selling it on to an increasingly paranoid consumer base. The situation is reminiscent of a scene from the classic Steve Martin film, *'The Jerk'*, where the hero lands a job as a weight guesser on a travelling fair. The hero is having 'issues' with handling the responsibility associated with handing out prizes and speaks with the fair owner, who informs him that to date he has taken numerous dollars and handed out 50 cents worth of crap. On understanding that the whole point of the exercise is to make profit, the hero, now brimming with confidence shouts something along the lines of, 'pay us some money and have the chance of winning some crap'. I'm probably sounding cynical here, but every time you eat a ready meal, or watch a DVD with a washed-up star in lycra, you are being totally ripped off. The only reason for the production of such shite, is for the producers and marketers to make as much profit as is practicably possible. This can be said also every time you go into the butchers or greengrocers to buy some raw ingredients. However, in such cases, what I feel is very important is that the buyer has greater control in terms of cost to profit ratio and ensuring what they put into their bodies is actually nutritious. It's probably fair to say that ready meal containers probably contain almost as much nutritional value as their contents.

The above having been said, it is important to note that the very nature of being the weight that you want, is not a 'quick-fix'; it requires a rethink of lifestyle. However, in my experience, the lifestyle change is not as drastic as it appears on paper, but there are some ground rules which must be observed in order to reap the required benefits.

**Weigh yourself regularly, every morning to start with.** This whole process will probably take less than 30 seconds of your day, but it is essential to set the tone for the day and helps you to stay focussed. I always ensure that I wear only a pair of pants when I weigh myself, so as not to distort the actual figure on the dial. When I get out of bed, this is the first thing that I do. If you follow this tip you will note that from time to time your weight will go up as well as down. However, the 'up' is only one or two pounds at a time and turning 'up' back into 'down' becomes easier and easier. Leaving it for a week or two, particularly with the type of lifestyle I have chosen to lose weight, could lead to numerous pounds having been gained between weighing myself, with the potential to lead to giving up and going straight to the cake tin for solace! As you change your lifestyle and lose the weight, it is important to keep a check as I have found that very quickly you can lose more weight than you require.

It could be argued that a daily visit to the scales is a little obsessive, and constant worrying about weight could lead to eating disorders. I would argue that visiting the pub could lead to you becoming an alcoholic, a visit to Syria could turn you into a Jihadist. Let's not piss about here, if you want to lose weight, you need a certain level of commitment. I recently watched a tv programme in the UK with the title something like 'what is the best diet for you?' The programme was hosted by a clinical psychologist and was riven with dieticians, nutritionists and a whole plethora of clever people wearing white lab suits and expensive spectacles. They had a preselected set of people on whom the programme was based, who had been pigeonholed into four eating categories. I immediately recategorised them all into one category: greedy, fat people! With the help of the clever people, the fatties were pursuing a new lifestyle and were filmed in their kitchen slicing carrots and weepingly expressing their gratitude for having been given the opportunity to 'see the light'. A number of them, during the course of the programme, fell apart and ran to the comfort of the local bakers to stack up on pastry, explaining that it was just too difficult to stay off the bad stuff. Another scene of hilarity came during the weekly weighing sessions that some of the subjects were made to partake in. Having been weighed, they would come away exhilarated, having lost two and a half pounds in a seven day period. Again, let's not fuck around here, it is possible to lose this amount of weight having had a decent shit! My take on all this very clever stuff is that the clinical psychologist and her band of advisors:

- Choose people of a certain disposition, or a certain percentage of such people, to make it look hard to lose weight. If they made it look easy (which it is) then they would be out of a job and the next series of 'You are far too thick to lose weight without being patronised' would never get commissioned.
- The clinical psychologist, although slim, and clearly very clever, probably has issues other than weight for which a tv series could be commissioned. Probably entitled 'I'm really shallow and I'm drowning in my own shit!'

**Avoid dairy products (most of the time).**

It occurred to me during a period when I was eating less and working hard, that I was still continuing to amass fat. I searched for the culprit and found milk. I wasn't drinking it by the pint, on the contrary, I was having it in my coffee, of which I was drinking numerous cups a day, which resulted in me drinking loads of milk by default! I still drink loads of coffee; however, I have switched from semi-skimmed, to skimmed. That's it!

I no longer have butter on toast, which, to the uninitiated probably sounds like 'hell'. However, given that I don't eat much bread anyway this is no great problem. You should try this. Avoid spreading butter, or any type of margarine or spread, on your bread or toast. Sure, have the other stuff otherwise you would be eating dry toast and even I agree that this is shite, to say the least.

My consumption of cheese, which used to be vast, has diminished, but I have not packed it in completely. I now class cheese as a luxury which, when consumed, is consumed with relish and enjoyed to the maximum.

Cream – you must be joking! Although as I will continually bang on, every now and again won't be of much consequence.

**Carbs!**

Bread, rice, pasta, potatoes. The very staples of life, without which, you, the reader, could not possibly face day-to-day existence. If you want to lose weight, then you better look at your consumption of carbs! Mine has not completely gone, however, I have taken a few simple steps to minimise their effects on my weight:

- Where possible, replace wheat with oats. I still eat a slice of brown toast now and again, but breakfast cereals are a definite no-go.

- If you have bread, for example sandwiches for lunch, make it a tortilla or a pitta and keep the quantity down.
- Rice, pasta or potatoes to be consumed in small quantities, no more than twice a week

**Alcohol.**

No rules here from me. Obviously, I wouldn't condone the reader drinking any quantities of alcohol. However my weight loss to date has included the consumption of as much wine, cider and beer as I have felt necessary to consume at the times in question. Please note however, I have never felt it necessary to consume 28 pints of lager every night for a period of six months. Three or four pints is more in line with the statement made.

Again, I can hear the experts condemning my alcohol consumption, stating that I should not be condoning its consumption to which I will argue, it's my life, I'll do what I want, as will the reader of this book (I hope). However, if ever I get a chance to write a book on alcohol consumption, I will definitely include a section of how the administrative classes (Chomsky again) are 'in bed' with the drinks' manufacturers, resulting in massive profits and totally unacceptable taxes being levied, based on supposed health and behavioural issues.

A fantastic illustration of the behavioural issues came at the recent Euro 2016 football championships held in France. In order to stop hooligans beating up on each other, the authorities, following the advice of experts (obviously) banned the sale of alcohol in certain areas. The biggest 'offing' to my knowledge at the tournament involved a Russian crew, who, it was reported consumed no alcohol and were totally combat trained and ready. The irony being, had they been pissed they may not have been so effective as a unit. Furthermore, on the subject of alcohol, France and violence, it would be interesting to see how many of those responsible for the recent terrorist atrocities were tea total.

### Naughty Things?

Chocolate, sweeties, cake and things of a similar nature come under the title of 'a little bit of what you fancy'. Sure, have a bit of chocolate but don't gorge yourself. After all, that's not what we are 'about'; what we are about is 'moderation'. One thing is for sure, if you stay committed and weigh yourself every morning, you will instinctively know when to allow yourself a naughty treat. Some people refer to this aspect of their life as a 'guilty pleasure', as if doing something that gives you pleasure is a crime. Let's be clear, it would only be a crime if you stole the shit in the first place, the actual gorging of it is no more than being a greedy fatty. There are numerous reasons fatties cite as being excuses for gorging behaviour, such as having to turn to chocolate to get over an emotional incident, or eating chips as a relief from boredom. Well, fatty, if you want to shed some weight you will need to turn to other things. In fact, why not dump the need to 'turn' at all and face the issue head on and get over it? Naughty things must include fizzy drinks, surely. Almost without exception, when reviewing the consumption habits of the really fat, the brown fizzy drink made famous by the Americans features quite heavily, except of course, in Scotland where this is substituted by a weird orange coloured drink that, let's face it Scotland, tastes like cold, fizzy piss.

**Eat to Live.**

Let's not pussy-foot around the issue, the unfortunate truth, no matter what the TV chefs or the supermarkets tell you, is that if you do not consume, you will die. This fact is not only true from a biological perspective, it also forms the basis of economics. Imagine a situation where the whole supply chain and our economic safety net disappeared overnight, the shops closed, the power stations shut down and your fridge was empty. What are you going to eat tonight, in the morning or indeed from now on? After three or four days, your pet cat would start to look tempting as a source of protein, particularly as the furry fuck has the ability to hunt for his own food, and the less you feed him, the more likely it is that he would fuck off, or indeed start to eat you!

As I repeat, I am not a scientist. However, a blind man on a horse in a snow storm, would undoubtedly see the blaringly obvious: **you eat to live.**

When I use the term 'live', please do not confuse this with the concept of life portrayed by the media, because that concept, which for all but a very small minority of people, is totally aspirational and in most cases unachievable. By live, I mean to get up in the morning and function as a human being. I agree that the speedboat, James Bond lifestyle looks very tempting, but remember this, even James Bond eats, drinks and shits and if Mr Fleming was of a mind to, he could have given James Bond the need to have a gastric band fitted, due to his frequent visits to the English chippy located on a high street in Monaco. It has been remarked upon that Sean Connery was looking a bit porky in his last appearance as 007. Perhaps they should have entitled this film 'You only eat pies'!

At the time of writing, a large rail workers' union in the UK is in the process of organising a number of strikes, based on two fundamental principles:

- Safety
- Work/Life Balance

Anyone who has worked for a living, particularly in the construction industry will have had safety rammed down their throats for as long as they can remember. The use of the 'S' word strikes fear into the hearts of everyone in and out of the workplace, with an industry having developed over the years to perpetuate this fear. This industry is 'the health and safety industry'. It is amazing, almost anyone, from any walk of life can attend a multitude of 'death by PowerPoint' events, undertake 'parrot fashion' exams and overnight become some kind of health and safety shaman. Every day in the UK alone, acres of paperwork containing snot are generated in a kind of 'uneducated leading the uninterested', an exercise in futility. The paperwork has been accepted as the way in which people are kept safe and almost everyone in modern society elicits a 'slide response' to the existence of this constructed reality and will listen to anyone who seems to know what they are talking about, even though they may, at the heart of it, think that that very person is a prick. Admittedly, there are some industries which, as part of their execution, there is a need for meticulous planning in order to keep everyone safe, that is clear. However, the need for society to consume the 'snot' and avoid the lawyers getting to them, that the safest of activities are required to be overseen by the 'safety evangelists'. Many years ago, I worked on the construction of a highway in Buckinghamshire, which initially involved what is known as a 'muck-shift'. A muck-shift involves the stripping of topsoil by large mobile plant, which, if you happened to be in the way, would crush you. As a safety precaution, the issuance of high visibility waistcoats was pursued to enable machine and plant operators to see personnel around them. Perfect sense, would you not agree? A very useful safety device in this instance. Now look at almost every construction site. Everyone wears 'hi-viz', even those fitting carpets! I was once told that tradesmen, such as carpet fitters, wear 'hi viz' so that they can see each other when passing around the site and more importantly they can be seen by the public! It's as if, since the invention of 'hi-viz', the world has been afflicted with a sort of 'people blindness' or more interestingly, the world thinks that by the actual wearing of the aforementioned, we are much safer in all situations. Likewise, you would surely agree that wearing a hard hat where there is no elevated risk of your head getting crunched, would be foolhardy. However, once again, everybody wears them. This 'slide response' approach to the perception of managing safety, in my humble opinion, utilises the 'problem-reaction-solution' approach adopted by cosmetic companies, advertisers and even government, to influence our way of thinking. Take the 'fatty-issue' as an example:

- **Problem**: up to 50% of UK adults are obese (not sure if that statistic is correct, but let's assume it is for the purpose of making the point) and numerous primary school children are going to die soon due to junk food and fizzy drinks!
- **Reaction**: 'Tonight on News at Ten, we expose the dirty bastard food producers and drinks manufacturers as they shovel sugar, fat and salt down the throats of prepubescent schoolchildren, and you, as parents should be very worried, because after all it's you who is letting this travesty happen in the first place!' This is usually followed by a comment from an ordinary person from the 'bewildered herds' reacting. 'Well, you know, I'm beside myself with worry as Gerta (camera pans onto a three-year-old the size of a bus) is not getting the nutrition she needs, and I feel helpless because the pizza, crisps, fizzy drinks and other shit I feed her daily is being loaded with calories. I think she and all schoolchildren of her age, are going to die tomorrow unless someone does something quick.'
- **Solution/s**: A minister announces a sugar tax, better labelling of food and other measures to protect our children's futures. A celebrity chef, famous for making dinners that would floor a fucking brontosaurus, announces a war on dinner ladies. The mega burger chain announces that they will, alongside their super calorie slop burger,

make bags of carrots available. That smart-arsed TV presenter, you know, the one, who looks amazing, has brought out a video diet and workout plan so even a fat twat like you can have a six pack!

We get this three-pronged approach time and time again and no matter what the results of one tranche of bullshit, there is always another on the horizon, because if there wasn't, we might free ourselves from the 'shackles of helplessness' and come to realise that if you eat and drink loads of bad shit, you will get fat!

The work/life balance is another, in my opinion, 'construct' designed to confuse the fuck out of the bewildered herds. The phrase itself infers that when you are at work, you are not 'living'. How can this be? You still breathe, think, eat and shit during work time don't you? The truth is that the 'living' bit, from the perspective of our current cultural norms, includes activities such as:

- Dancing while looking amazing to yourself and every other fucker. You will do this as often as you can because when you are doing this you are not at work and you are having a good time. Who knows, if you are lucky the person of your dreams will appear into your life, take you into the bogs and fuck your brains out.
- Drinking alcohol, because this helps you forget what a mundane worthless piece of biology you actually are. Fatties, in general, it has to be said, like this particular 'life activity', as it loosens their inhibitions and lets them have a 'good laugh'. How often do you hear fat women in

particular refer to themselves as 'bubbly', as opposed to being fat and up for a good laugh?

- Spending time with your family: Generally, I prescribe to family life and cannot really be disparaging, however, a look at the daytime TV shows and the media driven 'you're worth it' mantra appears to be in total opposition to any family values I hold dear.
- Taking drugs: it's amazing the lengths that some people will go to in order to escape the harsh realities of life. I have, in the past, taken all sorts of 'substances', generally on a social level and, it has to be said, had a good laugh on more than one occasion. However, my drug taking ceased many years ago, since when, the proliferation of drug taking seems to have gotten out of control in most sectors of society. It is noteworthy, that two drugs in particular have a dramatic effect on people's weight, namely heroin and crack cocaine. I do not pretend for one minute to be an expert. However, in my experience, 'junkies' tend to be skeletal thin. I can see Donald Trump and his mates dropping on that statement and accusing me of encouraging class A drug use. Let me be absolutely clear on this, I for one, having consumed all manner of substances in the past, would not recommend any substance that 'fucks you up' and based on the knowledge I have, it is fair to say that drugs such as heroin and crack cocaine, along with horse tranquilisers, genetically modified cannabis and all the other shite available on the black market will, in varying degrees, fuck you up! 'What then', I hear you say, about alcohol? Yes, absolutely, in my opinion too many people

are dependent on alcohol and, yes it is, or has fucked them up. A recent cultural norm which, it seems has proliferated amongst the younger members of society, is the practice of having 'pre-drinks'. To explain, we need to look at the culture that has arisen around the concept of 'the weekend'. The weekend, from a 'work/life balance' perspective, starts around 3pm on a Friday afternoon and ends about 7pm on a Sunday night. This is a time, for those lucky enough to work weekdays only, that you can forget about the fact that you have a job and indulge, guilt free in some of the activities alluded to above. For me, as a young man, this used to involve a Friday night dash from home to Oldham town centre to consume as much beer and possibly spirits as I could afford. A visit to a nightclub would ratify my actions, as the DJ would play records with lyrics extoling the virtues of 'the weekend' and, in some cases, documenting the singer's eagerness to finish work for the week. Forget about the fact that he works in a factory (or similar) and get out on the dance floor, as this is the one place that he, or she for that matter, can truly be free. I, along with generations of working people before me and since, have bought in to this concept. Take a look at any town centre on a Friday or Saturday night and the concept 'buy in' is on full display. I have spent many an evening gracing many town centres, off my tits, laughing and joking and having what I perceived to be a good time. For me, as I think it is fair to say for most people during the 70s and 80s, this concept was more social than alcoholic, in that it was the meeting of friends, who as the night wore on may, or may not get fucked up.

Nowadays, the social element still seems to pervade, however, groups of people meet up in their homes to consume quantities of hard liquor, to get fucked up, before they go out! It seems that being fucked up has become a 'badge of honour'! The drinks industry, who let's face it can only benefit from increasing alcohol consumption through their media outlets, put out the message 'please drink responsibly'. As if they give a flying fuck about ensuring controlled consumption of their products. Their message actually, through subtle advertising, is along the lines of: 'Drink our shit on a regular basis and you will not only have a fantastic life in spectacular surroundings, you will also get to hang out with, and fuck the person of your dreams.' It's funny, there are actually adverts that encourage pre-drinking, generally involving groups of women drinking cheap shit wine, given an exotic sounding name, identifiable with the strap line 'girls just want to have fun!'

Now, before I launch into the next point I want to make, I need to clarify something before your 'slide response' kicks in. I have, in the past, been accused of being sexist, racist, homophobic, a bully and all manner of 'ists'. I have come to learn, that in general by labelling someone, for example 'racist', the labeller then has 'free reign' to openly execute (generally verbally) the person, or group of people having been labelled. My absolute conviction is that someone, somewhere uses the slide response approach to manipulate society as a whole and get people to act in a way befitting whatever their agenda might be. It appears pretty clear to me that the 'chattering classes' appear to be the first element of society to pick up on this. For example, the mill town of Oldham saw an influx of Asian migrants of the Islamic persuasion during, as far as I know, the seventies. The indigenous population affectionately labelled these migrants as 'Pakis'. Around 1980, I moved from my 'working-class' environment into what I can now see as a 'middle-class' environment (from Oldham to London). I learned very quickly that all my cultural norms with regards to the 'incomers' were not shared by my new social circles. In fact, not only did they disagree with what I believed to be 'the case', my very mentioning of anything derogatory in this regard would be met with outright anger. Scroll forwards 40 years or more, it appears, so I am told, that certain elements of the culture brought to the UK all those years ago, wants to bomb the fuck out of every fucker. The chattering classes, at the time of writing, are struggling with this concept, now realising that through their 'slide response' approach to the subject they may have overlooked certain elements of the incoming culture that they do not necessarily agree with. For example, a slide response most common amongst menopausal middle-class women when confronted with Islam, is their distain regarding the emancipation of women. Please do not think for one minute that I condone it. However, I am constantly amused with the quandary that the middle-class wankers find themselves in, because let's not forget, 'girls just want to have fun' and when it comes to 'fun' the term 'girl' is a label that stays with some women until they are well into their 60s, with labels such as 'cougar' being bandied about, referring to menopausal women who actively seek young men to fuck. It's hardly surprising this cougar proliferation has become present in society as it appears that the media and advertising elements of society have targeted this demographic as an element of society that will spend money like it's going out of fashion, in order to 'look good', 'be worth it' and 'have fun'.

At the time of writing, there is an advertising campaign on national television for a large hotel chain which best illustrates the current thinking. Over the past few years, I have spent many nights in hotels operated by this chain and it has to be said 'you do get a good night's sleep'. However, the campaign referred to set's up two particular scenarios. The first involves a group of young men in their 20s and 30s, who are being sold the concept of being fit, eating large breakfasts with their mates and revelling in their own testosterone. This advert finishes with a line explaining that the men in question are scaffolders who, as can be clearly seen, are on their way to work. The second advert opens with a 'cougar' who, having said to whom I can only assume to be her child, 'look after your daddy for me', straightens her clingy dress, dries her hair and meets her buddies in the bar for sparkling wine. This advert ends with the group leaving the hotel, dolled up and about to get into the taxi that awaits them. Clearly the message here is that they are on their way to 'have fun' (whatever that might infer).

With the recent proliferation of social media, it has become the norm to publicise your life for the world to see. I must admit my failing in this respect and can see how addictive it has become to look at what everybody else is doing with, I suspect, a sort of sub-conscious peer review taking place to monitor my perception on my place on the planet. I make at least daily visits to a site that has recently started sending me frequent 'memories' which are basically photographs of me taken over recent years. Generally, the photographs involve me 'playing up' to the camera during some social event. The pictures from three or more years ago are of particular interest to me, as I can see how much fat I was carrying at the times in question. As I have stated previously, in my experience it is only on photographs that I am able to see how I actually look at any given time. When I look in the mirror, I tend to perceive myself exactly the same, fat or not fat. I'm guessing this is due to the cumulative effect of weight gain or weight loss. As I have indicated, my current weight loss lifestyle change has happened over two to three years, with my appearance changing very gradually.

The list of 'life' activities is endless, and in some cases, some people would argue that work is their life. However, regardless of how you may view the work/life balance, a fundamental basic rule exists. If you do not consume, you will die and no matter how much the TV chefs turn the activity of eating into an art form, you must remember that you 'eat to live'. Ask anybody resident in a besieged city, such as Aleppo for example.

Armed with the concept of eating to live, why then would anybody eat shite? Why not treat your body as a temple and feed it with food that you know is nutritious and is benefiting you? Why can you not understand that too much food, of the wrong kind, or even of the beneficial kind, will have some sort of repercussions, the former probably resulting in you becoming a fatty?

Again, I must revisit some issues before we move on as I, too, am a victim of the slide response syndrome, having been brought up with today's cultural 'norms' rammed down my throat. I referred to looking at myself in the mirror and on photographs, with the sub-conscious aim of a peer review. The opinions I make of my appearance, I reckon, are based on what I am told is an acceptable appearance by the media and other cultural mechanisms. It would be very difficult not to base your opinions on anything else. However, for most people, the aspirational images portrayed are generally put 'out there' to sell products. To align their products with people of exactly the right look and the perceived level of success should, from their perspective, result in maximum sales. The problem is, we are bombarded with so many of such images that, unfortunately, we have accepted them as the norm, with an ever-decreasing standard deviation from that norm.

It is important, if nothing else for your mental health, that you are clear on:
- Why it is you want to lose weight?
- What weight you will be happy with?

I have hovered around my target weight for some time now and have recognised that when my weight is less than it was the last time I weighed myself, I still get a positive feeling.

It is very important, I feel, that when choosing this type of lifestyle you remain absolutely clear in your own mind on the two questions above, at all times. The reactions I have received from my peers over the years I have discovered, have a bearing on the mental aspects of my lifestyle choice. A positive 'wow, you look great' comment has the obvious positive results and reinforces my resolve to continue. However, on occasion I have received comments indicating that I may have gone too far. Remember, those making the comments are subjected to the same cultural stimulus as you and their opinions will be based partly on their perceptions of themselves. This is why I feel it is very important to have a target weight and reasons to maintain that weight. Let me give you my reasons which exist at the time of writing (these may change as I experience more life).

- Relief of pain: as a middle-aged white man, raised on a Western diet, I was carrying a lot of fat. My knees ached, obviously from carrying too much weight and I suffered from constant back pains, which I attribute to my giant gut exerting lateral forces on my spine. Since losing the weight, neither of the above (touch wood) have been an issue. Again, I stress that I am not a medical practitioner. I am a normal bloke, who reckons he has taken control of his weight. I understand that illnesses attributed to being a fatty can be wholly, or in part attributed to genetic disposition, or just 'the luck of the draw'. However, as my peers and I race towards a box in the ground, I hear more and more: high blood pressure; heart problems; removal of limbs; blood clots; surgery on limbs; back problems; diabetes. Sound familiar? I may end up suffering from one or all of the above, however, at this moment in time at least I can say I have tried to do something about it.

- Buying Clothes: as you will have read above, I have, over the years suffered terrible anxiety over the purchase of clothing. As a youngster, I was never able to get exactly what I wanted, which, I suspect gave me the perception of never quite being able to conform. As I have got older the need to conform has diminished, as I can now see how 'shallow' this requirement is. In recent years, my need has been more of a financial nature and that of convenience. As an older bloke, it is always important, I feel, to have a couple of decently tailored suits. When I say decently tailored, I'm not referring to Saville Row, but more like your high street 'off-the-peg' affair. As a fatty, I was unable to get such an item from your run of the mill store; I had to visit a 'gentleman's outfitter' who was able to provide the 5 inch chest jacket and 4 inch waist trousers I required. I know that some people reading this have statistics way higher than that and so should be able to empathise with my sentiment. Once you deviate out of the standard deviation, say above 4 inch chest and 3 inch waist, you not only tend to pay more for your clothing, but the choice on offer to you is very restricted. I can hear the 'fat and happy brigade' shouting, 'I get my clothes online, from LAR-DASS.com at very reasonable prices and they have a massive range on offer.' All I can say to this is 'good luck fatty, I'm very happy for you.' My point here is, I no longer have a problem getting the clothes that I want and suffer no anxieties when partaking in the activity of clothes buying.

- A feeling of well-being: the fact that I'm doing something positive in terms of what I eat results, in some aspects of my life, in a more positive outlook. Another very important point I want to make regarding my experience is that I have, where possible, utilised everyday foods readily available from the range of food outlets at my disposal. I have not bought into some of the jaw-droppingly expensive fads, like drinking green slime twice a day. The 'green slime brigade' seem to be in a never-ending spiral of discovery, which involves paying extortionate amounts of money for foodstuffs which, in normal circumstances, would be used for cleaning pubic hair from garden gnomes (to quote Mike Harding). It amazes me that such people use food as a lifestyle indicator. Don't get me wrong, I don't begrudge people feeling better about themselves, it's just the constant 'banging on' and the total smugness of discovering something new and life-changing that gets my goat. A couple of years ago, a lady that I know was visiting a friend. The lady in question makes a living selling 'alternative stuff' to what appears to be those who can afford it. Being from the city and being accustomed to the recent pop up, street food fad, she mentioned on numerous occasions the fact that it had been days since she had consumed any 'raw milk'. I know it's quite obvious, but for those of you who don't know, raw milk is unpasteurised. When I was a child, when raw milk was the norm, it was decreed by those who know best that all milk consumed by the public should be at least pasteurised in order to get on top of the nasty diseases that can be passed on when you steal the foodstuff of a young cow/goat/sheep (in this case, I'm talking about cows' milk... smart arse). After listening to the lady in question for a number of hours, and being friendly with a local dairy farmer, I could bear it no more. I organised an early morning visit to a milking parlour, where she was able to get her hands on a litre of the product she so craved. What I found very interesting was, firstly, her horror at being put in the 'firing line' of the rear ends of 20 or so cattle, but on being handed a litre of raw milk she offered the farmer in question £3.50, asking whether that was enough. The farmer in question refused the money but informed the lady that in normal circumstances he would receive 18p for that litre of milk! This, I feel, is 'lifestyle versus reality'. There are actually people out there whose lifestyle choices are so removed from the day-to-day choices made by your average person that a whole culture has manifested in our more affluent urban environments where reality has become stilted to them. What is slightly concerning is that large numbers of those people with what could be described as having stilted norms, make up a large proportion of our cultural and media populous whereby they are able to convey their mantras to everybody, as if it is normal. How often have you thought to yourself 'I know what, I'll knock up a bread oven and a coffee roaster out of parts of an old washing machine, make artisan pizza and roast some Costa Rica Santa Anna'? When was the last time you ate down the local pier in a café owned by two celebrity chefs? How is your three acre organic vegetable plot doing? Sorry, I started to bang on a bit there; however, these people, nice though they are (and they are nice), only help to frustrate the average person on the street. (Did you notice I said person as opposed to man? This is because I believe that women to can be just as good at sports as men and for a male athlete to ask his female athlete girlfriend, 'what's for tea?' is very, very sexist.) Their aspirational, lifestyle mantras, entertaining though they are, do not reflect the realities of the normal mundane life choices available to those trying to pay their rent and feed themselves and their families. The good news, if you are a fatty trying to lose weight, is Guatemalan frog testicles are not necessary here, you can pick up what you need from your local shop or super market.

**Learn to Cook**

If there is one surefire way of absolutely ensuring that you eat healthy, nutritious life enhancing food, with control of every facet of your intake, then you must cook as much food, from scratch, yourself. Again, this is where the excuses, such as 'I can't cook' come flooding into the arena. For those who use this excuse, but who are able bodied, I would ask the following questions:

- Can you operate a smart phone?
- Can you operate a computer?
- Do you watch TV of an evening?
- Can you buy things from a shop?
- Do you want to lose weight and keep the weight off?

If the answer to any or all of the above is yes (this list is miniscule in comparison with the number of questions that could have been asked), then you can cook. In essence, cooking in order to become in this case slimmer, follows a few basic principles: you get hold of numerous food elements known as ingredients, you process them with various tools, one of which is referred to as a knife, you process them further in a container, let's call this a pan, while applying heat, usually on a thing known as a cooker. By following the above and taking the time to fine-tune the process you are able, very quickly, to produce what is known, the world over, as a meal. By trial and error you will find that very quickly, the meals resulting in your taking the time to learn, will not only be healthy and nutritious, but will also taste pretty darn good. I may come onto some recipes later on. However, I feel it prudent to make some important points at this stage on the subject of food:

- I have adapted my recipes over time according to my tastes with the underlying principle that I want to lose weight. It is important that you develop your own recipes based on your tastes, if this is to become a lifestyle choice.

- You will from time to time have to serve some of your food to friends and/or family. Ensure that you don't serve it as 'special food' which, in some cases, will result in mockery and a drop in your confidence. If they don't like your food, then fuck them.

- Be prepared to stomach things which at first you do not like, in the knowledge that: they are doing you good;

they are helping with your weight loss; and it is possible to acquire a liking for foods that at first taste like shit. Take stilton, for example. That having been said, if a particular food makes you vomit, or come out in a rash, then it's probably a good idea to ditch it.

- On occasion, and armed with your cooking prowess, throw your rule book out of the window and make a meal that fulfils all of your desires and have a meal that even the fattest fatty would be proud of consuming. If you are sensible, however, you will control the portion size and keep such an occasion as a special event rather than it being, for example, a daily occurrence. I would suggest once every two weeks.

- Take the time to cook and enjoy it. With practice and a bit of forward planning you can be pretty darn sure that almost every bit of food you put into your system is doing what you want it to do, which in this case is helping you lose weight and keep you alive and healthy.

- Finally, do not look at this as a 'DIET', something that will ensure that you can stop doing at a certain point in your life, only to go back to the life that you had before. My experience, which prompted me to write this down, lost me five stones in weight, in approximately ten months. I realise that I have to continue in principle with the lifestyle, however, my need to lose weight has now diminished and my concern is now to maintain my current weight (around 12 1/2 stone).

On the subject of cooking, probably the main excuse for not cooking is 'time'. Often the old 'I'm a busy mother/father trying to hold down my very important job I do not have time to cook.' (Funnily enough, I don't think I've ever heard those exact words, but you get my meaning?) This is probably the hard part for everybody. Unfortunately, you are going to have to find time to cook if you want this to work for you.

**Television!**

It was a wise man who penned the following rhyme: 'Television, drug of the nation, breeding ignorance and feeding radiation.' This could possibly be one of the biggest single contributors to the prevalence of the fatty. At the time of writing, I have just sat through a series of 'I'm a Celebrity, Get Me Out of Here!' This consisted of ten minutes of action, sandwiched between two party food adverts extolling the virtues of gluttony. Interestingly enough, out of the actors chosen to play the part of the gluttonous family members who seem to spend most of their time preparing and eating banquet food, not one of them was remotely overweight. Obviously, the advertiser would not want to give the general public the impression that gorging yourself on their crap may result in obesity, but let's be honest, it does! The point I wanted to make here is that sitting through this makes me hungry and it takes a lot of self-control to stay away from the pantry and remind myself that I don't need to eat, even though the television is telling me otherwise. For people with no self-control, the temptation to eat, without a second thought must contribute to their increasing waist size. What is even more thought provoking is, that if asked from where the weight gain has come from, most fatties won't be able to tell you, which, if you watch the fatty programmes on television this inability to pinpoint their weight gain reasons is usually followed by tears of self-loathing.

The truth is, television and now increasingly the internet, bombards the viewer with conflicting information on what they ought to do to live a full and rewarding life. It appears that, just as in Maslow's Theory of Hierarchical Needs, we all strive to move up the pyramid to 'self-actualisation'. It's almost like the religious amongst us, whose ultimate goal is to spend eternity in paradise. The problem being of course, is that due to the plethora of Earth-based religions, based on dogma and intolerance of other religions, if this paradise exists then I should imagine a serious issue with segregation and a continuation of 'our prophet was righter than your prophet'. If I eventually find myself up there.

I bring religion into the equation, as I believe it to still have a strangle hold on the lives of even the most atheist amongst us. As a baptised catholic, my parents sent me to a vociferously Protestant primary school, followed years later by an almost Protestant Third Reich secondary school. My impression, particularly of the secondary school, was that the teachers were bullies, which was borne out particularly in my case, as a constant recipient of corporal punishment. One particular point to be made here is that, particularly at secondary school, I was fat; which, in the less politically correct 1970s, caused no end of problems.

I remember that as a teenage fatty, who in my particular case was slow to biologically mature (the latter created all other sorts of anxieties particular in the changing rooms), my defence mechanism was to make people laugh. I found that being the comedian helped me integrate and make friends. How disappointed was I when, on numerous occasions, I lined up while my friends chose team members for a sporting activity such as football and was more than often than not the last to be chosen? (That type of think will fuck you up.)

The net result of my comedy was school reports, the like of which I look back on now with pride with teachers writing comments such as 'disruptive', 'unteachable' and the one I wanted to bring to your attention was from the gym teacher, who used to strut around the school in a track suit instilling fear into children and teachers alike:

'A satisfactory effort despite obvious obstacles.' This I read as, 'Your son tries hard, but gets nowhere because he's a fat fucker!' This comment was written about me 42 years ago and it's testament to my life ever since that I remember it word for word. There have been, in my lifetime, hundreds, if not thousands of times when my fatty status has caused me 'issues'. However, those six words created by someone who may have turned out to be a kiddie fiddler (bit harsh), have resonated and had a profound effect on my life ever since!

# DO NOT BECOME ANOREXIC!

You may recall on a previous page, I stated that you should weigh yourself every day. The vision of the scales going down in readings is very addictive with weight reduction being a 'good thing' and weight gain being a source of anxiety. This can become, if not kept 'in check', an obsessive disorder. You must remind yourself constantly that this is not a 'diet', this is a 'lifestyle choice'. For me, I have decided on a weight and size that I want to be and follow these basic rules:

- If my weight increases out of my target, I will take steps to get it back down. In this instance, two or three pounds would trigger this reaction.
- If my weight falls below my target, I will relax my rules for a day or two to bring my weight back up.

When weighing yourself every morning, you must remember the food that you consumed the day before is still in your system and this, too, has a weight. You will find, when talking small weights, that a visit to the toilet will shed pounds!

If you think for one minute you may have developed an eating disorder, then get professional advice!

**Give yourself at least one day a week to eat what you like!**

For me, Sunday is the day I try to have a good breakfast and, of course, a Sunday roast.

# WHAT SHOULD I EAT THEN?

The following chapter illustrates what worked for me. However, you may find that replacing my recipes with other weight loss beneficial foodstuffs. To be honest, there is no point in me 'spoon feeding' you (excuse the pun) with exactly what to eat and when. If you have got this far in the book, then you should realise that you are on your own. If you are depending on me to run your life then you need to question your ability to do anything. Take control for fuck's sake! I'm sure you will get a food plan that works for you if you look hard enough.

**Breakfast**

Porridge made with skimmed milk. Try to avoid the microwave stuff, particularly the type with dried fruit in it, as this tends to be highly calorific.

Or

Scrambled egg and sliced ham – no bread, but an oat cake is a fantastic alternative.

One or two, but no more, piece/s of wholemeal toast, no butter with jam, honey or peanut butter. I said earlier that no bread is the way to go. However, this is just one slice, so stop accusing me of being fickle and get over yourself!

Anything, which you know contains few calories.

I could bang on about slow release of energy or making sure you have a 'good breakfast' as it will set you up for the day. Remember, if you are a coal miner, which is highly unlikely as the UK government has closed them all, then a full fry up would suffice. However, if you work in a call centre or behind the stick of an excavator, you are likely to be sat on your arse for a large part of the day and that fry up, or more importantly, the culmination of numerous fry ups will give rise to the process of fat accumulation and you will inevitably become a fatty!

Kippers! Definitely one of my favourites. Don't have 40 of the fuckers in one sitting however!

One day of the week, or even two if you feel like it, whatever you want. Go on, knock yourself out, after all 'you're worth it'. Did you see the irony there?

I'm sure that the experts amongst us will see that the list above is quite sparse and the word 'boring' might spring to mind. As stated above, I am not an expert and I'm sure that some smart arse will deliver a list of gargantuan proportions. Eat what you want at breakfast, but remember, most people don't have the luxury of time at breakfast, as displayed on the UK soaps and I find that foods like those mentioned above are quick to make at home and available in hotels, for those of us who are unlucky enough to have to work away from home. Do a bit of research and discipline yourself!

You will find that having had a breakfast similar to the above at say 6.30am, by 9 or 10 am you would gladly eat your shoes. This is where you need to start working. I find a cup of tea or coffee staves off the hunger, but not for long. In times of desperation I use a banana or one of those oat granola bars to stave off the hunger. I have found over the latest weight loss event:

- If you keep busy, then, although hunger pangs are there, they disappear.
- After a few days of using willpower, it will get easier to control your hunger.
- Giving in at the first sign of hunger will make the whole process more difficult.
- If you focus you will lose weight and if you are a major fatty, you will be surprised at how much weight you will actually lose.

There is a very important point to make here: if you are like me, you will give in to temptation on occasion, when for example, a giant chunk of chocolate cake is thrust before you due to the fact it is somebody's birthday, or similar event. Have it if you want! It's not the end of the world. If you want to lose the weight and keep it off, you will need to realise that this is a 'change of life' and as long as you stick to the main event, the odd cake/pie/burger should be no problem. Since my lifestyle change, I have made frequent visits to the famous burger chain, you know, the one with a clown as its mascot. On almost every visit, I have, to put it lightly, gorged myself stupid, knowing that, further on down the line I will need to resume my chosen regime. For some of you, this paragraph may be a 'ray of hope' in that you can see that there are naughty things you can eat. However, be under no illusion, you will, on occasion have to abstain when offered that meat pie, just as an alcoholic would refuse a pint of vodka.

Once again, cut down or cut out:
- Bread
- Pasta
- Rice
- Cheese
- Pies
- Full fat milk
- Potatoes ... and all the other things that you know make you fat.

I have spoken with many fat people over the last couple of years regarding what they should do to lose weight. Once I start to go through the 'list', their persona tends to diminish as they mentally start to examine how they will be depriving themselves. I find that I am having to justify my regime in a way similar to the following:

Take spaghetti bolognaise, for example. The dish comprises a meat and tomato sauce mix (good stuff), pasta (bad stuff) and parmesan cheese (bad stuff). If you are true to the regime, then you eat a bowl of bolognaise, or two if you like. That's it. Another example would be a Sunday roast. Have everything, except potatoes and Yorkshire pudding. You will see from the two examples above, I myself have 'fallen into the trap'. I am justifying the regime by using quantity to demonstrate that it is not about depravation.

Now, if this book ever gets onto the shelves, I am certain that there will be all manner of nutritionists and professors decrying the pitfalls in my diet regime and informing you that all kinds of ill health will beset you unless you 'eat a balanced diet and get regular exercise'. I agree! However, if you are going to shift the fat, you are going to have to do something and this is what I did, without a PhD. I have to say, over the years, one of the funniest things I have seen is when fat nutritionists stand in front of the television cameras advising the general public on what they should eat.

Remember also that advice on what you should and shouldn't eat changes weekly. For example, I am writing on the very day that the World Health Organisation has announced that processed meat and red meat is as 'deadly' as asbestos and cigarettes.

**Lunch**

This is a particularly difficult time of the day in that this is where, if you are not careful, it is easy to consume numerous unnecessary calories. For those who lunch at work, it is particularly difficult, as we are told (and I tend to agree) that if you don't consume at this time your performance in the afternoon will dip. I am reminded at lunch of, in my experience, fat office women, who are generally bubbly (fat) wear big flowery print clothing (to hide the fact that they are fat, usually to little avail) and who bring in skip-sized containers of salad to work (to convince themselves and others that they are trying to lose weight). In general, the salads themselves contain so many calories, an elephant would struggle to keep its weight down and more poignantly, these women must consume vast amounts of the 'wrong stuff' either side of their midday salad, as they never seem to get any thinner. For me, lunch is generally 'on the go' and usually comprises:

- A couple of homemade tortilla wraps.
- If eating in a canteen, meat and veg (no carbs).
- A sandwich, or a piece of flan. Always, if possible, homemade and always a sensible portion.
- If buying from a vendor, one of the above or something like falafel.

The list above may sound pretty boring and is full of anomalies, such as consuming pies and bread. However, as you get into your own regime, you will get to understand that if you make as much of the food as you can yourself, you can control your weight and as long as you maintain control of what you eat at all times, you could add a pre-prepared salad to the list and lose the weight.

**Dinner**
- Meat and vegetables
- Fish and vegetables
- Vegetables

That's it! With the ingredients above, and a little practice and know-how, you can concoct all manner of delicious foods, remembering at all times to cut out, or minimise:
- Carbohydrates
- Sugar
- Dairy

So, for example, if by using the above I make a curry, I will add lentils to the main event (to bulk it out), omit the rice and may have a tortilla wrap.

Every Friday for many years, I have been food shopping with my long-suffering legend of a wife. Since the weight control lifestyle, our shop has become simple and generally very nutritious. Usually when we get to the store, I have eaten very frugally the whole week and exposure to all the food on offer leaves me ravenous. The answer to this problem, for me, has been simple: our next stop after the shopping is done is the local burger chain, where my order is almost without exception:

A regular cheeseburger, a 'feature burger' (normally about 800 calories on its own), regular fries and, get this, a diet cola! The meal, once consumed, amounts to about 2000 calories, two thirds of what I am told to consume per day. This may be. However, more often than not, my daily calorie intake is far less, so I'm guessing it balances out.

I don't really prescribe to counting every calorie, however, having a rough count up as you go through life, in my experience, does help with the weight loss and exposes the fact that those small things which a lot of people regard as snacks, are loaded. For example, there is a famous high street bakers, famous for cheap fresh baked produce. My particular favourite of their products is a Cornish pasty, which I can usually consume in about four mouthfuls. I was shocked to find that they contain 750 calories and that eating two, for example at lunch time (a common event in my past life), amounts to half the recommended daily calorie intake. Put a fry up and a spaghetti bolognaises either side of this and you are consuming more than you are burning. This will quite obviously, if continued as a lifestyle, will make you fat and if you are anything like me, you will not realise that you are gaining weight, or more to the point, not even care, until the moment arrives that you will finally admit to yourself that you are a fatty and you feel it is time that you did something about it. That's probably the reason that you are reading this book?

# SOCIETY

You will probably have gathered by now, I am of the opinion that there is an inextricable link between society, peer group perception and the individual that has given rise to the explosion of fatties in the so-called developed countries of the world. It appears that, no matter how rational we think we are being, there always seems to be a higher, more corporate entity pulling our strings and making us what we are. It is amazing, given the number of free thinking individuals there are on the planet that we should all, or so we are led to believe have almost exactly the same opinion of what is right or wrong. It is true that if you thrust your hand into a fire, you are likely to get burned and this will hurt. I'm sure there is a world consensus on this topic, however, I can hear the smart arses proclaiming, 'what about those tribesmen who walk on hot ashes?' Ok, you have a point, but they are not going about their daily lives, they are just showing off!

My perception of what is right or wrong, in terms of the opinions I form about different topics, are borne out of nurturing by my parents, coupled with both their and my education. In 1967, I was thrust into the world of education and it was from that point I feel I was indoctrinated into the world of ceremony and perception. As you may have gathered, my upbringing was working class and on reflection so was my education. The town in which I was born and raised existed to spin cotton and the mainstay of its inhabitants at that time had been educated to serve this function. This has been affectionately known as 'factory fodder'. The rise of unions, which in itself is a whole volume of books, had made it comfortable for the factory fodder, who marvelled at their inside privies and hot running water and some, in the upper layers (financially speaking) of the factory fodder even had aspirations of the concept of being 'middle-class'. We are often told that, as a society, the only fair way to coexist is through the system of democracy, a political system giving voice to everybody it serves. The question is, does democracy serve us, or do we serve it? Currently in the UK, we are in the throes of what the 'sound-biters' have affectionately named Brexit, which, as we all know doesn't refer to a breakfast cereal, but to the UK (what is left united of it) having a democratic vote, which resulted in our government pulling the whole nation out of something that has become known as the European Union. The UK first entered this Union in the early 1970s and my understanding is that the idea was to improve the trading opportunities of the member states, as well as keeping checks on countries who fancied their chances at world domination. The news media, it appears, worldwide, is obsessed by Brexit. My questions regarding this whole circus are this: who was it that decided we were going into Europe in the first place? Whose idea was it that we should leave? I know we had a referendum, however, there weren't massive anti-European demonstrations demanding Brexit, or sieges of the Houses of Parliament demanding our democratic right to have a referendum. No, we were told we were having a referendum and spoon fed the facts from both sides of the spurious argument, in what we are told is democratic debate. The period leading up to the referendum, and the time ever since, has led to constant banging on about the rights and wrongs of something for which I believe we have absolutely no say, regardless of our social media profile. You will have read earlier, and probably surmised that I am a big fan of Noam Chomsky, who as I write has referred to Donald Trump as the death knell of the human species. (Now that's a quote!) His description of democracy not only explains a number of unanswered questions about who runs the place, but adds fuel to my fire of how corporations view humans as 'consumption units'. He, as I think I referred to earlier, describes the general population as 'the bewildered herds'. This category generally includes the working and middle classes. The theory is that they are fed bullshit and confusion, resulting in bewilderment and in a number of cases, anger. You only need to go back to the 1970s and look at the political landscape of Jamaica to see how manipulation of the bewildered herds got results for those who required them. The second category he describes as 'the administrative classes'. These I perceive to be the few that break out of bewilderment and those who were born into the position of administration. The public schools and those with close ties to the royals I believe to make up this category. This probably explains why Winston Churchill's first parliamentary seat was in a constituency in Oldham. I probably stand to be corrected, however, I thought the whole idea of democracy, was that it came from a 'grass roots' level, with groups of people electing one of their peers to represent them in The House of Commons? I'm not sure, but as far as I know Winston Churchill wasn't revered for his clog dancing prowess, or ability to consume vast quantities of black pudding, so how was it then that the likes of him got to represent, in parliament, the type of people to whom he had previously referred to as rats? Taking this into consideration and reading Chomsky in your spare time, might lead you to believe that, as with most things political, we are being sold 'a pup'! The final category in Chomsky's theory is the ruling class. I have only a sketchy idea of who I think they may be, however, if you read the conspiracy theories, they usually point in the direction of the British Royals, the Zionists, the Masons, or even some other worldly reptilians, all of who are looking to downsize the world population in order to enslave it. I'm not sure how true this is, however, my interests lie in the fact that there is potentially a ruling class who oversee all this bullshit, as it is they, who in my opinion have a lot to answer for.

My education, as well as preparing me for manual labour and aspiration also indoctrinated me into the ceremony of worshiping God. Now, I would like to say at this point that my indoctrination has been so entrenched, that even though it has never been proven to me personally that a God exists, I still have a suspicion that there may be some truth in it. I am not a religious man per se, however, almost everything I know about the subject of God, has come through the ceremony of standing, sitting, singing and praying, which in the early years involved me having to put my hands together and close my eyes. This I did nearly every day in perfect unison with my classmates. Then, at the weekend, my social life as a youngster involved the boy scouts (more praying) and the obligation to do it again on Sunday in the local church. My indoctrination was through the Anglican Church, who, for numerous reasons make me sceptical as to their qualifications to be the link to God. My local church was affiliated with my primary school. The vicar, who visited our school during religious events (such as Christmas and Easter), was treated with the utmost reverence and, to me as a small child, the garb worn by this 'man of God' gave vision to this most holy of men. He, along with our teachers, would give sermons and guidance to us on mortals and the rights and wrongs of life. One of the most memorable tools of indoctrination was the ramming down our throats of the Ten Commandments. This was done regularly, almost akin to the parrot fashion way we were taught our times tables. The Ten Commandments, in my opinion, make a lot of sense. After all, murder, theft and coveting your neighbour's ass can't be a good thing. Imagine then, my confusion when the man revered by me and my peers as being the route to heaven, gets caught fucking the cub mistress; who also happens to be the mother of one of my classmates, and the wife of the local coalman! I am not really a Catholic, although I was baptised one, so I guess I am. However, what I have heard of the actions of priests and nuns against children is sickening, I think that is a no brainer. My final example came later in life, during my time working as a construction consultant. For a few months, I worked on a project in Gloucester, for a client whose name was The Ecclesiastical Insurance Company. I'm not exactly sure of the actual statistics, however, I recall that in 2005, this little-known (to me) entity ranked as number three in the UK in terms of size. The company, it seemed, were/are so wealthy that the project that we were working on was actually a sacrificial office building (not lamb); its purpose was simple. If, for whatever reason, the main office block (HQ) became unusable, say, for example, in the case of a fire, the company could just relocate immediately and continue functioning normally. This was in 2005. However, I'm sure that today, due to their heavenly connections, they use cloud technology. (See what I did there?)

In summary, and based purely on my experience of the Anglican Church (I discount all other religions in this next statement as I have little or no experience and also The Salvation Army because I perceive them to be good people), I feel it necessary to point out that, although there are a lot of well-meaning people involved in the organisation, there is enough evidence to surmise that they are a bunch of 'wrong-uns'.

What then, I hear you ask has all this got to do with me wanting to lose weight? Good question! It is my firm belief that if you are going to be happy with the weight you are, or the way that you look, you need to understand that it is you, and you alone who will make this happen. The corporations, politicians and other entities on which we base our opinions, in my humble opinion, are rife with anomalies, which, if explored objectively start to make you question their validity or purpose. As seen above, the part of the book which, in the run of the mill fad diet books would give you the magic formula (prescribed diet plans and exercise routines), leaves it to your imagination and encourages you to take control, rather than depend blindly on the words of someone who may be under the endorsement of others. As I have repeated time and time again, I am not a dietician, however, I have managed, quite easily, to get to and maintain the weight and statistics (in terms of clothes size) that I am happy and comfortable with and my point is, that you can too, if you believe in yourself and understand that in a number of facets of our day-to-day existence, society 'feeds us a pup'.

As I ranted on about above, the media, it seems, has a specific agenda to frighten the general public into behaving in a certain way. The current pattern seems to involve frightening different sectors of society into hating each other, to the point that war appears to be just around the corner. Interspersed amongst this message of impending doom are other 'worry bombs', such as the sad state of the national health service, the obesity crisis and, of course, the global warming nightmare. Most of these issues, from my individualistic perspective are, to a certain extent, out of my control. Yes, I can recycle, I can avoid going into certain areas of town and can become a weekend eco warrior. However, on Monday morning, I will still be required to take some mode of transport to generate income for myself in order to live, which unfortunately will expend some of the finite resources available on the planet. If I were to act in a totally eco-friendly way immediately, then it would be a matter of days before I have to resort to stealing food, which, in the eyes of the law, would make me an undesirable member of society. Another issue from a societal perspective, would be my inability to generate tax revenue. I understand as a society, if we are going to have any kind of public cohesion, there are things that need to be done and to enable those things to be done, a public purse needs to be generated and maintained. As an individual member of this system, I seem to be being taxed on every penny that I earn, every penny that I spend, every vehicle I drive and, notwithstanding this, I will be taxed when I die (death duty)! Again, it is my humble opinion that the media uses subtle ways into, firstly, making me blindly conform to being taxed from every angle and secondly, into making me think that the people with control over the purse strings give a flying fuck what I think about how they spend it! Every day we are bombarded with the administrative classes referring to the hard-working families who seek value for money from the taxes that they pay. I'm not sure on this one. However, the money we spend (us hard-working families that pay taxes) on a Royal family surely doesn't represent value for money? Point of note here. When, on the occasion these parasitic fuckers appear in public, you know, when they shake hands with the peasantry, or wave at us from a posh car or balcony, how many of them do you see that are morbidly obese? Surely, given the amount of privilege they have at their disposal, at least one or two of them would be showing signs of being a fatty? The more astute of you may spot the odd one with a big gut, however, I don't recall a situation when one of them has had to be craned onto a balcony to undertake their civic duties. Why then, do we have the poorest sectors of our society, so fat that they stop traffic, are not allowed a single seat on a plane, or are being refused hospital treatment? My firm belief is this is due to not purely what they eat, it is moreover, what they are fed. A number of years ago, I read a very interesting book entitled 'The Welfare State We're In'. The book compared and contrasted issues such as housing, health and education from a pre and post welfare state perspective. Statistically, the book eloquently explains, as a nation we were much better off before we became utterly dependent. This is a very simple and sweeping generalisation, however, it appears that large sections of our society are dependent almost entirely on the state for their whole lives. This dependency is, as is clear, not confined to the so-called welfare scroungers who, we are told, derive from families who have not worked, or paid taxes for three or more generations. No, we have and keep a massive public sector of those who are in work with gold-plated working conditions along with a growing army of public sector pensioners, for whom, the so-called 'black hole' in their pension pot, is not an issue, as their pension pot deficit is underwritten by those hard-working families who pay their taxes. A great number of the public sector pensioners retired at the age of 55 and as well as drawing from the pot, swathes of them have taken other jobs and/or draw the state pension as well. Meanwhile, those workers not in this dependant situation have no such privilege and have seen their pensions ravaged by the government, a government who incidentally are made up of personnel who benefit from public sector pensions. I may be being a bit cynical here, however, if you were the MP responsible for work and pensions, would you want to keep the lid on the fact that a whole sector of society is, in effect, 'milking the system' and he or she is as busy in the milking parlour as anybody? If this travesty did appear prevalent in the public consciousness, would it not appear to be hypocritical that he, or she, had the bare-faced cheek to accuse the peasantry of not finding work, particularly when you analyse the current work climate?

Take any former industrial town, such as Oldham, or Treorchy. As stated above, Oldham was born out of the need for an industrialist, or industrialists to make as much money as possible out of spinning cotton, whereas Treorchy came to being as a result of another financial speculator, or speculator providing a need for coal. You will note I referred to the towns as former industrial, due mainly to the fact that we are told that we now live in the post-industrial era. A rose-tinted reflection of our industrial past saw the labourers from the countryside moving into an urban environment and fuelling the industrial revolution which, we are led to believe, made Britain great. Notwithstanding the poverty and shit working conditions and exploitation, let's stay romanticised and imagine the building of houses and infrastructure and the formation of proud working-class communities based on cotton and coal. Those proud working-class people, were in some cases, so proud, that they paraded themselves under banners, illustrating an affinity with their place of work and their comradery with their union brothers and sisters. Some of the financial speculators, whose need for factory fodder was so great, built their workers decent housing and communities for which any peasant would be proud to be a part of. Then, due to numerous contributory factors, the need to spin cotton in Oldham or dig coal from the valleys, diminished and as I write today, I think it is fair to say, has completely disappeared. We must remember at this juncture that cotton, as far as I am aware, is still required, likely in larger quantities due to the growing world population and coal, regardless of climate change, is still burnt. All that aside, however, from an objective perspective, the very reason for the existence of the towns in question and the glue which held the communities together has disappeared. It is true, there are opportunities to take up other vocations, increasingly in what has become known as the service economy. However, if what we read is to be believed, the digital revolution will and is demolishing the chances of anyone to make what has come to be known as 'a living'. How then can it be that an MP, who we have already established is on-the-take and who represents a system which I suspect serves those who administer it, publicly bad mouth those in society who, for reasons that I can sympathise with, do their utmost to avoid making a living from flipping burgers (shit food for the masses again) or sitting in a call centre being abused from disgruntled members of the public like me? Another interesting book, entitled *'The Singularity is Near'*, examines the recent developments in technology and illustrates the exponential advancements in areas such as artificial intelligence (AI). The Singularity in this instance, loosely speaking, is the point at which machines and technology make human involvement in production all but obsolete. Take a look at a typical car plant or food processing facility. Robotics and automation have increasingly taken over, much more efficiently it has to be said, from people. I have spoken with my father on this topic many times, who, quite rightly, has pointed out that this technology needs people to make and maintain it. Although in the short term (the next ten years) I, in my humble, opinionated way agree, I would argue that due to the quality of production and AI capacity of what we will have moving forwards, it is not inconceivable that the machines and technology will soon have the ability to make and maintain themselves. What the fuck, I hear you say once more, has all this talk of robotics got to do with me losing a few pounds? Once again, as an individual, I think it is important to stick to the facts of life. If you consume too much of the wrong stuff you will be a fatty. A nation, any nation on the planet, has needed a healthy population to sustain its needs. Its needs, from where I am standing, have been to work, generate profits for someone and pay taxes. Those of you who, in the past have seen television classics such as 'World at War', will recall the old black and white film archives of the Germans partaking in mass gymnastics, in a bid to keep fit and healthy for the Reich. While all that propaganda and lemming behaviour was going on, the German government presented a vision of the future to their loyal citizens. Again, being very general, the idea was that as a member of this great socialist state, you paid some extra taxes into a pot which, it was portrayed, would be invested in massive leisure complexes to which the 'hard-working citizens' of the Reich could drive in their VW beetles. All of this came free, as part of the package. For reasons far too complex for my simple economic prowess, when it came time to 'pay the piper', the 'cupboard was bare'. It appears that that little Austrian bloke with the daft 'tash' and big attitude, had 'spunked' all the cash on rockets and big houses in the Alps. The point is, all this talk of artificial intelligence, the decimation of the industrial towns, the historical evidence that the rulers don't really care about the peasantry and the explosion of morbid obesity through the consumption of shit, leads me to believe that many members of the peasantry are eating themselves to death and, by doing so in increasing numbers, will decrease the existence of their kind. At present, were the people, a lot of who would come under the banner of 'Chavs' along with others with, shall we say a religious leaning, to become aware of some kind of conspiracy, then, the differences between them, which on the whole are superficial and based on lifestyle choice, would diminish as they come to realise that they are all in the 'same boat'. If this were to happen tomorrow, the riots that one and all keep on predicting might just happen and those who the conspiracy theorists have been pointing at for some time, would come out of the shadows, with who knows what consequence? If you were one of those people (if indeed they do actually exist), would it not be a whole lot easier if you gave the peasantry shit to consume and just enough to fulfil their aspirations and, in time, they would fight and consume themselves to the point of extinction?

You might, as a result of reading the past couple of pages suspect that you are reading the ramblings of a mad man, but please, do spare me the ability to inject some artistic licence to illustrate an important point:

If you are prepared to take what you are given, without question, or any kind of input (such as work) because you are happy taking the easy option then good luck with the diet, Fatty. However, if you take on board the 'bigger picture' and the fact that with just a modicum of input and thought from you, as an individual, into the things you consume, it is highly likely that you will achieve your objective of losing, or indeed gaining, the weight you desire. My deriding of everything public and corporate, is merely added to 'the mix' to illustrate the potential for it all, as far as each individual is concerned, to be counterproductive to the aspirations we are all supposed to aspire to. (I'll shut up now as that sounds a bit cheesy!)

I could not, however, complete this work without trying in some way to connect the 'arts world' to all the ailments of society, including obesity. I have no real affinity with art per se, in that, on the whole, art, in all its diverse mediums is something that I, as an individual, can take or leave. Take paintings, for example, be they by the Grand Masters or by some mediocre present-day portrait painter, I may look at them, gain some kind of mild pleasure at the skill involved in producing them (less so in the latter of my two examples) and then move on. Music, be it contemporary or classical, some I like, some I learn to like (it grows on me) and some I think is shit. Note, however, I am not skilled to any extent in production of, or consumption of art in any of its forms, but I am aware that if I do, or do not like a particular piece of art, the immediate and long term effects on me as an individual, are less than zero. In short, I suppose what I am trying to say is, 'art does not really matter'. It will come as no surprise to you then, if I were to describe the art world in general as a load of old bollocks, full of self–aggrandising half-wits, who, in a number of cases, command far too much for the tosh that they produce. The producers of this tosh, are made to feel infinitely important by those who surround them, such as those who pay breath-taking amounts of money for something that in the real world amounts to something you might hang on a wall to hide a stain. The economic benefits of the arts are often portrayed in the media as being a substantial percentage of our GDP. This as may be, however, the art world itself pervades an air of exclusivity in that lesser mortals don't buy in to certain concepts because they do not understand them. I have come across this bullshit on numerous occasions in both artistic debate and another of my biggest issues, wine. I, it has to be said, am a regular consumer of red wine and while not an expert, I do realise that some of the cheaper varieties on offer in the supermarket (which is where most of my wine comes from) are, to me unpalatable (to use a wine snob's vernacular). There does, however, become an issue from my perspective when comparing the value of wine in currency. Now I know there are particularly good vintages and price is relative to vintage and availability, that is basic economics. I do take issue, however, when undertaking taste tests with wine snobs comparing an £8.00 bottle of wine, with a bottle of say £100.00. When struggling to justify the difference in price range, given that the taste and, therefore, the enjoyment are almost identical, I have been met with sneers and, again, the impression that what is so blatantly obvious to me, utilising my sense of taste, is incorrect due to my lack of intellect. I remember once, during my twenties, sat in a shared house full of artists, being made aware of an event of great, life-changing significance. The event in question was a video screening (to an excited audience of artists) of a Japanese film by an influential and important Japanese film director. The film was entitled, *Ai No Corrida*. For those 'in the know', this title refers to a sexual act resulting in a heightened level of sexual gratification (very loosely explained). The film, as it unveiled itself to the audience was, as I proclaimed at the time, hard core pornography which, had the film been called Fist Fuck Tokyo, my artistic chums would have agreed wholeheartedly. However, my 'knuckle dragging' reaction to what was clearly a fine piece of artistic work, was met with the same, self–aggrandising, pompous reaction. It couldn't possibly be pornography (which appears to be a bad thing to the art squad) because it was art. I have a similar issue with one of my in-laws who, as a piece of wall art, has a tray on the wall over her Rayburn (how very middle class). The picture on the tray is of two young scantily clad prepubescent girls, I think the term is nymphs. The older girl appears to be trying to persuade the younger girl to perform some sort of act, while the younger girl gazes straight at the artist while displaying a kind of naïve smile. As a viewer, my immediate reaction is that the older girl, who has been molested previously by the artist and his mates, is in the process of getting her sister or her mate initiated into the whole paedophile experience. If this scene were to be recreated through another artistic medium such as photography and the artist was a council tenant from Ipswich, the police would be drafted in and the artist would be in solitary confinement as we speak, to protect him from the other prisoners. In the case of this picture, however, it could not possibly mean anything as sinister as my inference because it is art.

Art, in the form of movies, television and radio have been, up until the recent emergence of IT media, a source of artistic consumption to the masses for a number of years and movies, in particular, have helped shape our society into what it has become. The people involved in the movie industry, particularly the big stars have, there is no doubt in my mind, been and continue to be influential in the shaping and acceptance of social norms. I imagine that the likes of some of the screen stars of the 20th century were responsible for the younger generations to take up smoking in order to be a rebel just like the hero that they had consumed. I imagine also that, in this particular scenario, those who were in the business of making profits from the production of tobacco products, could see the marketing potential and as a result shovelled skip loads of cash into the making of movies. If this were to be true, after all this is just me theorising, then the art of movie making could, as a by-product of its existence, be another way to influence the consumption of the bewildered herds. This could be one of the reasons that people who, for a living fanny around pretending to be somebody else, get paid a shed load of money and another example of why, if you are going to achieve your goal you need to view these things for what they are, just entertainment, which, may have some underlying corporate or political agenda attached to it designed to influence your behaviour. As for the art world itself, as a whole, I think the analogy of *'The King's New Clothes'* best describes my conclusions. You may recall the fairy tale of a King so pompous and gullible that he is tricked into paying a fortune for some clothes which didn't actually exist. On trying on these 'non-clothes', the King decided to parade himself through the town. Initially, the bewildered herds, who could clearly see the situation, refused to do so, for fear of looking silly. This scene continued until a young lad, unfettered by the general bullshit of life, proclaimed 'look everybody, the king is bollock naked.' Once made aware of what was right in front of their nose all along, the crowd began to mock. On the subject of what is front of your nose and taking things at face value, does this mean that anything preceded by 'Her Majesty's' is owned by the Queen? I'll let you ponder on that one!

# WHERE TO GO FROM HERE?

If you have managed to get through this little number, may I congratulate you for your tenacity and dogged determination; it must have driven you mad. As I have probably banged on about a number of times, I am no expert and I have no pretentions of ever wearing a lab coat for a living. I have, however, lost enough weight and have maintained my weight loss for a number of years, to the point that I have felt smug enough to write a book (all be it a short one) about it. If you take nothing else away from my ramblings, please note that I have wanted to purvey the following key messages:

- You can lose the weight that you want by eating sensibly; quantity of food consumed is not always the main determinant, it is the quality.
- You need to learn to cook, or take the time to cook and ensure that you consume in such a manner so as to achieve your goal.
- Keep an eye on your weight.

- Do not look at this as a diet or fad and remember, most of the pricks out there selling this snot do so predominantly for profit.
- Do not be one of the bewildered herds and remember your success is up to you.
- Remember, you can lose a significant amount of weight just by visiting the toilet.

Good luck and on the subject of 'those who run things', take the words of Robert (Bob) Marley with you in his song, '*Guiltiness*' (a track on the Exodus album).

'They would do anything to materialise your every wish.'